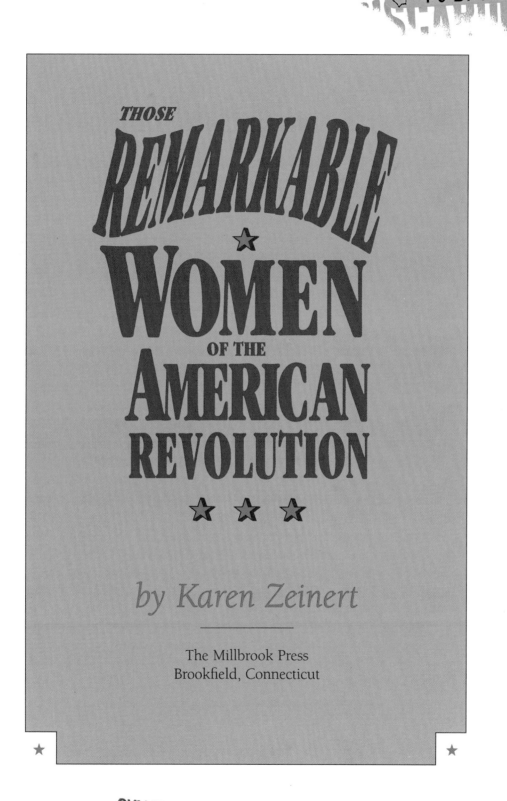

THOSE REMARKABLE ★ WOMEN OF THE AMERICAN REVOLUTION

★ ★ ★

by Karen Zeinert

The Millbrook Press
Brookfield, Connecticut

Photographs courtesy of the Library of Congress: pp. 7, 21, 27, 36, 40 (bottom), 45, 64, 81; *Rachel Weeping* by Charles Willson Peale, 1772, Philadelphia Museum of Art: Given by the Barra Foundation, Inc.: p. 9; Rhode Island Historical Society: p. 18; Frick Art Reference Library: p. 28; Historical Society of Pennsylvania: pp. 33, 54, 85; North Carolina Department of Archives and History: p. 40 (top); Bettmann: pp. 48, 58, 63.

Library of Congress Cataloging-in-Publication Data
Zeinert, Karen.
Those remarkable women of the revolution / Karen Zeinert.
p.   cm.
Includes bibliographical references and index.
Summary: Examines the important contributions of various women, Patriot and Loyalist, to the American Revolution, on the battlefield, in the press, in the political arena, and in other areas and shows how they challenged traditional female roles.
ISBN 1-56294-657-9
1. United States—History—Revolution, 1775–1783—Women—Juvenile literature.   2. Women—United States—History—18th century—Juvenile literature.   I. Title.
E276.Z45   1996
973.3'15042—dc20   95-47609   CIP   AC

Published by The Millbrook Press, Inc.
2 Old New Milford Road, Brookfield, Connecticut 06804

CONTENTS

A Woman's Role

Teach her what's useful, how to shun deluding;
To roast, to toast, to boil, and mix a pudding;
To knit, to spin, to sew, to make, or mend;
To scrub, to rub, to earn, and not to spend.

The Evening Post, a colonial newspaper

In late June 1782, a dozen mounted colonists loyal to England's King George III charged into a small Continental Army camp near New York City. These Loyalists were determined to kill the thirty-one Patriot soldiers resting there, and the attackers quickly unleashed a volley of musket balls, which sent the soldiers scurrying for cover. Although the Loyalists had the element of surprise on their side, once the soldiers were in position, they proved to be so strong that the raiders were forced to retreat.

As the attackers rode off, the soldiers began to pick up the injured so that they could be taken to a doctor at a nearby army camp. All the wounded eagerly accepted help except twenty-one-year-old Robert Shurtleff, who had a nasty gash on his head. Unlike the others, Shurtleff repeatedly begged his comrades to leave him alone. Believing Shurtleff wasn't thinking too clearly because of his head injury, the men ignored his pleas. They rounded up a horse, put Shurtleff in the saddle, and began a 6-mile (10-kilometer) trek to the doctor's tent.

When the men reached the tent, Robert had little choice but to accept some medical attention. However, he deliberately concealed a serious wound in his thigh, planning to take care of it himself when he was alone. By doing this, Shurtleff avoided undressing, which prevented the doctor from finding out that the "man" he was treating was really a woman in disguise—a woman named Deborah Sampson who feared discovery so much that she was willing to risk dying to protect her identity.

And it's no wonder that Sampson was fearful. In 1782 it was thought absolutely unacceptable for a woman to costume herself in men's clothing or to take a role that colonists thought only a man could play, such as going to war. As a result, Sampson believed that if her true identity became known, she would face ridicule and rejection from both her comrades and the public.

In addition, Sampson had every reason to believe that she would be severely punished if she were unmasked. When Deborah first filled out enlistment papers in early 1782—enlisting then as Timothy Thayer— her unusual way of holding a quill caught the attention of a woman in the office who knew Sampson. This woman told army officials that Thayer wasn't what he pretended to be. Furious at being duped, the officials sought out Sampson, tore up her papers, and warned her to stay away from the army—forever. Shouting and waving their fists in the air, the officials told her that if she enlisted again and was caught—and they assured her that she would be—she could expect no mercy. She should, they snarled, put on a skirt and behave like a respectable woman.

———

The vast majority of American colonists, like the men who threatened Deborah Sampson, expected women to behave in a certain fashion in the

Scandalous, outlandish, and totally inappropriate: Any woman in colonial times who stepped out of her acceptable female role and into a traditionally male role, like that of soldier, could expect to be labeled this way. Some women were bold enough to take it a step further than this character in an eighteenth-century book by disguising themselves as men.

1700s. Colonial women were supposed to marry, raise a family, manage their households efficiently, and, above all else, obey their husbands. Women who did not wed were thought to be avoiding their social responsibility, and were looked down upon. One colonial newspaper summed up the attitude of the day when it described an unmarried woman as "one of the most cranky, ill-natured, maggotty, peevish, conceited, disagreeable, hypocritical, fretful . . . never-to-be-pleased, good-for-nothing creatures . . . on earth."[1]

Because colonial society had many tasks that needed doing and was desperately short of workers, women were expected to have many children. Most wives gave birth to between five and eight offspring, but some had as many as fourteen. By having large families, colonists hoped that at least some of their children would reach adulthood—no easy feat when diseases such as smallpox and typhoid fever claimed the lives of at least one third of all children before they reached the age of three.

Colonial wives were very busy women. In addition to feeding, bathing, dressing, and supervising their sons and daughters, they had many household tasks to perform. How much time domestic tasks took depended on the family's income and where they lived. Women on farms, especially those far removed from colonial cities, had limited opportunities to buy manufactured goods such as fabric, soap, and candles. Also, because farming seldom produced great wealth, country wives had little money to spend. Instead, they had to produce almost everything they needed in their homes, as did poor city women.

Most finished products required many steps. In order for a woman to produce wool cloth, for example, she had to secure wool fleece, wash it to remove dirt and debris, card it to draw out long fibers, spin the fibers to turn them into a strong yarn, dye the yarn (using a homemade dye), and then weave the fabric on the family loom. Needless to say, when family finances permitted, fabric was one of the first products to be purchased by women.

Women in colonial times led hard lives. Children, who were
important both as members of the family and as contributors
to running the household, often did not live past infancy. Here,
a mother mourns the loss of her child to smallpox.

Performing the many chores proved to be an exhausting job. One woman wrote in her journal, "It has been a tiresome day. It is now Bed time and I have not had [one] minutts rest."[2]

An extra hand in such a setting was highly desirable, especially when wives were pregnant. Girls were taught to help their mothers (and train for future wifely duties) at an early age. If daughters weren't available, women turned to families of friends or neighbors. Sometimes parents from poor households would place a daughter in someone's home, where she performed a number of chores in exchange for food and shelter. Deborah Sampson, for example, was placed in a minister's home when she was ten years old, and she remained there until she was eighteen.

Although using children was obviously inexpensive, most girls needed lots of training and supervision. A mother's load could be lightened more easily if adult help could be found. Since most colonial women were busy with their own households, colonists whose income could be stretched a bit hired poor women in England who would agree to become indentured servants. These women were brought to the colonies at their employers' expense, and they agreed to work without wages for a specific number of years, usually seven or more. More than 80,000 women became indentured servants during the colonial period.

Some wealthy women in the New England area and most women who lived on large plantations in the southern and middle colonies seldom relied on indentured servants to help with their multitude of tasks. Instead, these women used slaves. Even though buying slaves was a very expensive proposition, owners who did so could count on steady, trained workers for many years. Like other women, slaves were expected to have children, for this increased an owner's wealth. Unlike other colonial women, slaves always faced the horrible possibility of having their children taken from them and sold to strangers, never to be seen again. At the beginning of the Revolution, there were 500,000 slaves in the colonies; approximately 150,000 of them were women.

Plantation mistresses were still in charge of the household no matter how many slaves were present, and these mistresses were expected to have the necessary materials on hand so that the slaves could do their jobs. This required careful planning, since most plantations were many miles from suppliers, and a quick trip to a nearby store to buy cooking utensils or flour or cloth was simply out of the question. Most materials were brought to plantations only a few times each year, according to orders placed by owners, who sometimes found the amount of paperwork staggering. Seventeen-year-old Eliza Lucas, who ran three plantations in South Carolina while her father was away, wrote in a letter to a friend, "I have the business of three plantations to transact, which requires much writing and more business . . . than you can imagine."[3]

Although most wives had control over household chores, married women had little voice in anything else. It was a common practice in the 1700s to treat a husband and wife as one person, not as two separate individuals. Logically, one person has only one mind, and the law gave the right to exercise that mind, or all decision-making power, to the husbands. This meant that unless a wife-to-be had lawyers draw up special papers that gave her the right to control any property that she might bring to a marriage (an inheritance from her parents, for example), her husband owned and had the right to control all property during their marriage.

Since men were expected to make the decisions, most colonists believed that women needed little education other than how to run a household, which they learned at home. Therefore, few girls attended school for any length of time. Most were taught how to read, however, usually by their mothers, so that they could study the Bible.

Even though most girls were not educated beyond being able to read a little, a few girls were very well educated for the time. The majority of these privileged few were members of wealthy families that had servants, giving daughters some leisure time. Also, well-to-do families often hired tutors for their sons, and daughters were allowed to attend some sessions when time permitted. On rare occasions, girls who worked as servants might also learn from these tutors. Deborah Sampson, for instance, was allowed to attend such sessions, which were held for the boys in the family she worked for, because her employer believed strongly in education for everyone. Deborah learned enough to be able to become a teacher, and she taught school for several years before she enlisted in the army.

Although it was difficult to do, some women also managed to become successful at business. On occasion, a husband might teach his trade to his wife—printing or minding the store, for instance—when he needed an extra hand in the business. If the husband died before his wife did, his widow sometimes was able to take over the family business and make a success of it. Some single women took the skills their mothers taught them and turned them into a business. They started fancy needlework classes, took in sewing, and set up classes for young children. Some colonial women ran shops that sold sewing supplies. By the time the war began, approximately ten out of every hundred businesses in Boston, one of the colonies' most prosperous cities, were run by women.

In the 1760s, hostility intensified between Britain and the colonies, and this would have a great effect on many women's lives. Most of the hostility was caused by Britain's refusal to give colonists a voice in how taxes were determined. Colonial leaders repeatedly protested, declaring "No taxation without representation!" Strapped for cash, King George III and Parliament refused to listen.

Colonial leaders then made plans to force British leaders to give them a greater voice in how they were governed. One plan was to stop importing British goods. Because many of these goods were household items purchased by women—fabric, candles, and soap, for example—colonial leaders knew that such a boycott would not be possible without the support of the colonial women. Not only would women have to be convinced not to buy British goods (the only goods allowed into the colonies), they would again have to manufacture everything they needed or do without. This was not good news to women who would have to return to their spinning wheels and looms.

To encourage women to do their part, officials held public spinning bees, and women who participated were treated as heroines. The publicity surrounding such events guaranteed that the women would get the king's attention, and this was pretty heady stuff for wives who had no voice in public affairs.

While some women gladly joined the boycott, shopkeepers who sold imported goods were more than a little nervous at the thought of empty shelves. Anne and Elizabeth Cummings refused to sign a pledge saying they would not sell British goods. When a local committee called on them, insisting that they join the boycott, Elizabeth was indignant. She accused the committee of trying to injure "two industrious Girls who ware Striving in an honest way to Git there bread."[4]

Hostility between Britain and the colonies increased in the early 1770s as King George and Parliament tried to tighten their hold on the colonies to eliminate any possibility of resistance. This upset the colonists even more, and to show their anger they held more protests, some of which turned violent. They also began to stockpile weapons for a possible rebellion. In 1775, armed clashes took place at Lexington and Concord, Massachusetts, when the British tried to find and confiscate some of these weapons. These clashes marked the beginning of the Revolutionary War.

Not all colonists supported the rebellion. Historians estimate that of the approximately two million white citizens in the colonies then, approximately one third of them joined the Patriots, about one third tried to remain neutral, and another third supported the king.

Loyalists supported Britain for several reasons. Some, especially plantation owners in the South, had strong economic ties with Britain.

Not only could they sell their rice and indigo for top prices in England, but the king granted bonuses to producers who could raise bumper crops, bonuses plantation owners did not wish to lose by joining a revolution. Some Loyalists were employed by the crown as royal governors, judges, tax collectors, and customs officials, and a successful revolution meant that they would lose their jobs. Most Loyalists, though, such as William Franklin, the royal governor of New Jersey and Benjamin Franklin's son, felt a strong loyalty to the royal family that was simply unshakable.

Although most husbands and wives supported the same side, as was expected, not all did so, and this caused some bitter arguments. One husband became so angry at his wife that he included a special provision in his will ordering his heirs to make sure that he and his wife were not buried side by side. He did not want to see his disobedient wife's face on Judgment Day, when, according to his religious beliefs, tombstones would roll away and the dead would rise.

The Revolutionary War was fought in all sections of the colonies as well as on the frontier. And as the Patriots and the British crisscrossed the countryside trying to gain the upper hand, many women became involved in the war. In some cases, soldiers brought the horrors of war literally to women's doorsteps when bloody battles were fought on their farms or in their villages or armies on the move tried to ransack homes, hoping to find desperately needed food and money. With husbands away in the army, militia, or Loyalist brigades, wives and daughters then had little choice but to take action on their own to protect themselves and their property. Some were overwhelmed by the decision-making involved and by their lack of knowledge. Others courageously defied traditional roles, as did Deborah Sampson, to help their side win.

These women played an important part in the war, and their dramatic contributions made all colonists reconsider what a woman's proper role should be—no small feat, even for the remarkable women of the American revolution.

In the Army

I'm not afraid of the cannonballs.

Sarah Osborn, camp follower

When war broke out between the colonies and Great Britain, recruiters for the Continental Army tried to enlist as many soldiers as possible. Unlike the American wars that would follow, this war began without the colonies' having a standing army. Desperate for manpower, recruiters were not too fussy about the men they enrolled. Boys as young as fourteen could enlist if they had their parents' permission, and men of any age were accepted as long as they appeared able to fight.

Recruiters usually set up shop on the busiest corner of a city or village. Surrounded by colorful pennants snapping in the wind and drummers and fifers who played rousing marching music, the recruiters fired muskets—or even cannons if they had them—to attract passersby. Once a crowd had gathered, recruiters gave their best patriotic speeches, sneering whenever they mentioned the king's tyrannical laws.

Although recruiters were concerned only with enlisting men, many colonial women were affected by the recruiters' spectacles as well. Some, like Deborah Sampson, signed up after disguising themselves as men and served as soldiers. Most, however, decided to become camp followers when their husbands enlisted, marching with the army as well as cooking and performing other duties for the soldiers. No matter what role the army women assumed, they were a committed, feisty lot. Sampson, for example, continued to seek active duty as a soldier even after she had been seriously wounded.

How many women fought in disguise is impossible to determine. Few—if any—would have confided their true identity to those with whom they served, and social pressure would have kept many from admitting that they had fought after they left the service. Therefore, historians have only been able to positively identify a handful in addition to Sampson: Mary Ritchie; Eliza Veach; Sally St. Clair, who was killed on the battlefield; and a mysterious woman who enlisted as Samuel Gay and rose to the rank of sergeant before she was discovered and dismissed.

However, historians believe that more than these few women served as soldiers. These historians point out that women's patriotic feelings and desire for adventure were not likely to have been any less during this war than in other conflicts in American history, when many women served in uniform. For instance, in the Civil War, when it was still unacceptable for a woman to join the army, records indicate that at least four hundred women fought on the battlefields.

Historians also point out that serving in disguise was probably easier during the Revolution than it would have been in other conflicts. Young women simply passed themselves off as teenagers who hadn't yet begun to shave or speak in a deep voice. These women bound their chests to flatten them, tied back their hair, and wore the most shapeless men's clothing they could find. If they were careful, they really weren't likely to have their true sex revealed until they chose to do so or until they needed medical attention.

Deborah Sampson's identity wasn't revealed until the second time she was taken to a hospital. After being struck down by yellow fever in Philadelphia and close to death, comrades carried Sampson to a Dr. Binney's tent for treatment. When Binney removed Sampson's shirt so that he might better hear the soldier's heartbeat, he discovered that his patient was a woman. He then took Deborah to his home, where his wife cared for her.

When Deborah was well enough to rejoin her regiment, Binney gave her a note to give to her commanding officers. This note told the men that Robert Shurtleff was a woman. The officers, understandably shocked, refused to believe the note's contents until Deborah changed into women's clothing. Instead of the punishment Sampson expected, she received an honorable discharge from the army. This treatment was due, in large part, to the way she had conducted herself on the battlefield, for she had earned the respect of the men with whom she had served.

Women who enlisted as soldiers were rare. On the other hand, women who joined the army as camp followers were a common sight, for about 20,000 women were followers at some time during the Revolution. Rumors were rife about prostitutes marching with the army, but in reality, the vast majority of camp followers were soldiers' wives who had no way to support themselves while their husbands were away at war.

While female soldiers were unacceptable and discharged when discovered, camp followers were often welcomed. This acceptance was due to the fact that followers performed traditional feminine chores: Besides cooking meals for their husbands and many other soldiers, they also did the men's laundry and nursed the sick and wounded.

Camp followers, unlike soldiers, were not paid. Instead, they were given rations—a half-ration for themselves (half the amount of food a soldier would be given) and a quarter-ration for each of the children accompanying them.

Women marched behind the soldiers, often in a very disorganized fashion. On occasion, General Washington ordered them to take a

Deborah Sampson was spared the harsh punishment she expected for impersonating a male soldier, and actually received an honorable discharge from the army.

different route when passing through towns so that his army might appear more professional in the eyes of the locals who gathered on the streets to watch the troops go by. Many of the camp followers considered themselves an important part of the army—which they were—and they deeply resented being thought of as an embarrassment.

One colonist watched the soldiers and camp followers being separated as they entered his village. "They were spirited off into the quaint, dirty little alleys and side streets," he wrote, "[and] they hated it." He added, "The army had barely passed through the main thoroughfares before these camp followers poured after their soldiers again, their hair flying, their brows beady with the heat, their belongings slung over one shoulder, chattering and yelling . . . and spitting in the gutters."[1]

Pregnant women and officers' wives were sometimes given rides in wagons. But even when transportation was provided, following the Continental Army as it moved through the colonies was no easy task, for marches were seldom short, easy jaunts, as Sarah Osborn found out when her husband re-enlisted as a sergeant in New York in the winter of

1780. According to her lawyer's statement made in court when Sarah was seeking a pension from the army:

> [Sarah] in [1780–81] in sleighs accompanied her husband and the forces . . . to West Point . . . [where] she and her husband remained till the departure of the army for the South.
>
> When the [men] were about to leave West Point and go south, they crossed over the river to Robinson's Farms and remained there for a length of time . . . recrossed the river in the nighttime into the Jerseys and traveled all night in a direct course for Philadelphia. [Sarah] was part of the time on horseback and part of the time in a wagon.
>
> They arrived at a place [near] the Schuylkill [River] where . . . they encamped for the afternoon and night. Being out of bread, [Sarah] was employed in baking the afternoon and evening.
>
> They continued their march from day to day till they arrived at Baltimore, where the forces . . . embarked on board a vessel and sailed down the Chesapeake [Bay] . . . until they had got up the St. James River as far as the tide would carry them.
>
> They marched immediately for a place called Williamsburg . . . [Sarah] alternately on horseback and on foot. There arrived, they remained two days till the army all came in by land and then marched for Yorktown.[2]

Sarah's trip from West Point to Yorktown covered more than 300 miles (483 kilometers).

Although followers remained in camp while the soldiers fought, these women and their children were still in great danger. Furthermore, when battles became furious, some of the cooks headed to the battlefront to help their husbands, becoming in the process what were known then as "half-soldiers."

One of these half-soldiers was Mary Hays, whose brave actions are believed to be the source for the legend of Molly Pitcher. Mary, whose nickname was Molly, followed her husband to his camp in New Jersey. In addition to her usual chores, she carried water in large pitchers to soldiers on the battlefield, earning the name "Molly Pitcher."

On June 28, 1778, more than one soldier took notice of Molly when, without apparent fear, she remained at her husband's cannon during the Battle at Monmouth Courthouse in New Jersey even when the enemy's fire became intense. According to legend, Molly didn't begin to fire away until her husband, overcome by heat and exhaustion, fell to the ground. However, an eyewitness, Private Joseph Martin, claimed that Molly and her husband worked as a team throughout the entire battle. He recorded his observations about Molly in his journal:

> [She] attended with her husband at the [gun] the whole time. While in the act of reaching for a cartridge and having one of her feet as far before the other as she could step, a shot from the enemy passed directly between her legs without doing any other damage than carrying away all the lower part of her petticoat.[3]

Private Martin then noted that Molly looked at her torn petticoat with little concern and, ignoring the obvious danger she faced, continued to fire her husband's cannon.

Another heroine of the battlefield was Margaret Corbin, who was also called Molly. When her husband enlisted in the Pennsylvania artillery, Molly prepared to follow him. On November 16, 1776, John Corbin's regiment was attacked by powerful enemy forces at Fort Washington, New York, and he was killed on the battlefield beside his cannon. When Molly, who volunteered to carry water to the battlefield, realized what had happened, she raced to her husband's gun and repeatedly fired it until one of her arms was nearly severed at the shoulder by grapeshot.

One of the most enduring legends of the
Revolution, Molly Pitcher is often depicted as a
larger-than-life heroic figure. Her true identity
has been disputed by some, but she remains an
important American folk hero.

Shortly after, the greatly outnumbered Patriots at Fort Washington were forced to surrender, and Molly Corbin was held as a prisoner of war for a brief time.

The Continental Army was only one armed force in which Patriots could serve; more than 150,000 men joined local militias, such as the Minutemen, which helped the army when it was in the militia's area. Women helped local militias by warning members about the enemies' movements in the area and caring for the wounded.

Some, like sixteen-year-old Sybil Ludington, rode through the night to rouse militiamen to battle when the British arrived. Throughout the winter of 1776–1777, militiamen near Danbury, Connecticut, had gathered and then hidden foodstuffs and tents intended for the Continental Army. Late in the afternoon on April 26, 1777, 2,000 British raiders, tipped off by Loyalist spies, proceeded into Danbury, intent upon destroying the supplies.

Shortly after the British arrived, the head of the Connecticut militia sent couriers racing toward the homes of local militia leaders. Sybil's father, one of the local commanders, was asked to gather his militia of four hundred men and march to Danbury. While it was too late to save the supplies, the courier said that it wasn't too late for revenge.

Sybil volunteered to alert the men, who were scattered along a 40-mile (64-kilometer) route. Riding her favorite horse, Star, she went from farm to farm, pounding on doors with a long stick to attract attention. When someone answered the door, she shouted "Muster at Ludington's!" and raced on to the next house. Her horse stumbled several times, and twice Sybil had to leave the road to hide when she heard other riders approaching, fearing they might be Loyalists. She was exhausted by the time she completed her three-hour-long ride, but she was heartened when she saw the number of militiamen prepared to march when she reached her home. These men, with help from other militias, caught up with the raiders and exacted a high toll from the British troops.

———

Like the Continental Army, the British Army and its hired soldiers, the Hessian mercenaries from Germany, also had many camp followers. Most of these women sailed from England or Germany with their husbands when they were shipped to the colonies. In the beginning of the war, British troops had approximately one camp follower for every eight soldiers; the Hessians had one for every thirty mercenaries. Four years later, the number of both British and the Hessian followers had doubled, due largely to the soldiers' practice of marrying colonial girls.

The sight of British camp followers angered and appalled the colonists, even those who supported the king. Poor and hungry, some camp followers stole food from colonial homes as they followed their husbands. Word about these thefts spread throughout the colonies, and British camp followers were greeted with hostility and suspicion wherever they went.

In addition, colonists were shocked by how the women were treated and by their wretched appearance. One of the women who lined the streets to watch the followers pass said, "I never had the least Idea that [God] produced such a sordid set of creatures in human Figure . . . great numbers of women, who seemed to be the beasts of burden, having a bushel basket on their back, by which they were bent double, the contents deemed to be Pots and Kettles, various sorts of furniture . . . some very young infants who were born on the road, the women [barefoot], clothed in dirty rags."[4]

British and Hessian camp followers could remain in the colonies only as long as their husbands were able to fight. The first shipload of widows and orphans was sent back to England in the summer of 1775, only a few months after the war started. This ship also contained severely wounded soldiers, who would never again be able to fight, and their families. This vessel was only one of many that would carry grieving survivors and victims of battle back to England or Germany during the war.

Not all foreign camp followers lived in poverty, though. Officers' wives had a far better life than did most camp followers, and these women often followed not out of economic necessity but out of duty. One of these was the Baroness Frederika Charlotte Luise von Riedesel, the wife of a Hessian officer. When her husband left Germany to fight in the colonies, Frederika remained behind to give birth to their third child, a daughter. A year later, she finally managed to secure passage for herself and her children to Quebec, where her husband was stationed. While she followed him, she lived in houses, usually offered by Loyalists.

In the fall of 1777, shortly after the baroness and her children arrived, her husband, by then a general, was ordered to join British forces near Saratoga, New York. Frederika kept a journal of her experiences in America, and some of her passages about Saratoga show her great fear for her husband's safety, a fear every camp follower must have experienced:

> On October 7, my husband, with his whole staff, had to break camp. This moment was the beginning of our unhappiness! I was just taking breakfast with my husband [in his tent] when I noticed . . . a great deal of commotion among the soldiers. My husband told me that they were to go out on a reconnaissance, of which I thought nothing, as this often happened.
>
> I had hardly returned to my house, when I heard firing, which grew heavier and heavier until the noise was frightful. I sat in a corner of the room shivering and trembling. The noise of the firing grew constantly louder. The thought that perhaps my husband would be brought home wounded was terrifying and worried me incessantly.
>
> Finally toward evening I saw my husband coming; then I forgot all my sorrow and had no other thought but to thank God for sparing him![5]

Ten days later, the British and Hessians were forced to surrender at Saratoga, and General von Riedesel was among the six thousand men taken prisoner. Once surrender terms had been worked out—the soldiers would be sent back to Europe if they promised not to fight again—the general sent for his family.

Although the baroness was afraid of what lay in store for her if she joined her husband in the American camp, she quickly realized that she and her children would be treated well. She recorded her arrival in her journal. "While riding through the American camp, I was comforted to notice that nobody glanced at us insultingly, that they all bowed to me, and some of them even looked with pity to see a woman with small children there. I confess that I was afraid to go to the enemy, as [being a prisoner of war] was an entirely new experience for me."[6]

The von Riedesels were given lodgings in various homes in Cambridge, Massachusetts, while arrangements were made to send them to Europe. The baroness endured her captivity better than did her husband, who suffered from serious bouts of depression. In fact, Frederika found so many things to her liking in the colonies that she named her next child, a daughter, America.

Loyalist militias, like the patriot organizations, also had female supporters. Among the most colorful and daring of these women was Flora MacDonald, an immigrant from Scotland. Flora had once saved the life of Prince Charles, a royal Scot who had led an unsuccessful uprising against England in 1746. She had helped the prince escape from the English when the revolt was crushed at Culloden by disguising him as a woman and leading him to a secluded harbor where he boarded a waiting ship and sailed for France. When the English realized what Flora had done, she was arrested and confined for a period of time in the Tower of London. In 1774, Flora and her husband, Allan, who had experienced serious economic difficulties in Scotland, joined ten thousand Scottish immigrants living in North Carolina, where she was regarded as a heroine.

When the Revolution began, British governors in the colonies eagerly sought out Loyalists who would form local militias or join the British Army. The governor of North Carolina asked the Scots in his colony for their support. This would seem to be an unusual request, since the Scots and English were old enemies. However, after Culloden, the Scots were forced to swear an oath of allegiance to the king of England, an oath they took very seriously. In addition, the Scots were very angry at the men who led the Patriots in North Carolina. These men, in the eyes of the Scots, had systematically seized power for themselves over the years at the expense of the poorer people. As a result, the Scots feared—and in some cases detested—the Patriot leaders.

So when the royal governor of North Carolina asked the Scots to fight for the king, Flora rode throughout the area, encouraging every Scot to support Great Britain. At least fifteen hundred agreed to bear arms for Great Britain, and on February 1, 1776, these men, wearing kilts and playing bagpipes, began their trek toward the coast, where they were to join British soldiers. On February 28, the Scots were stopped at Moores Creek Bridge by local Patriot militias. More than half of the Loyalist troops were taken prisoner, including Flora MacDonald's husband and son.

The battle at Moores Creek Bridge effectively ended the Scots' attempt to help the British, even though the war was far from over. Flora was forced to leave North Carolina when the MacDonalds' plantation was seized by a local Patriot committee. She sailed to British-held New York City in 1778, where she was reunited with her husband when he was released in exchange for Patriot prisoners.

Even though the Scots no longer openly backed the king, loyalism in the South did not die. Many Southerners, inspired by Flora Mac-Donald's courage, continued to support Great Britain until the end of the Revolutionary War.

Martha Washington (1731–1802)

Among the officers' wives who were camp followers of the Continental Army was Martha Washington. Martha had a large plantation in Virginia to run in her husband's absence—he returned to Mount Vernon only twice in the eight years he led the army—so she could not follow the general all year long. But Martha did join the army during the winter, when the responsibilities of both Washingtons were fewer.

Since Martha did not immediately follow the soldiers when the Revolution began, Loyalist rumormongers said that she was opposed to the war. As a result, on her first trip to army headquarters near Boston (1775–1776), Martha was occasionally jeered and booed by small crowds who recognized her as her carriage passed through their city. These demonstrations shocked Martha and appalled her husband. Martha put an end to these rumors when she reached the Continental camp and voiced her support for independence.

While in camp, Martha did what she could for her husband and the soldiers. To cheer the general, she brought along a carriage full of some of his favorite relishes and jellies as well as a generous supply of cured hams. She also helped him with his correspondence and made copies of important records. When time permitted, she knit socks for the soldiers, mended clothing, and visited hospital tents, trying to bring cheer to the wounded and comfort to the dying.

Because Martha was the commander in chief's wife, she was expected to put on a show of confidence even during the darkest days of the Revolution. This was a difficult role to play, and although Martha gave a good performance, at least judging by the comments of others about her, in private she agonized over the war and the danger her husband faced. Not only did he risk death on the battlefield, as did all combatants, but Martha feared that if the colonists lost the war, her husband would be hanged for treason—an unspeakable humiliation.

Faced with the difficult task of being the woman supporting the most prominent man in the Revolution, Martha Washington played her role with strength and character.

Lydia Darragh was an enterprising woman who
used her neutral Quaker status to gain the trust of
the British officers who met in her family's home. She
used this trust to acquire important military secrets,
which she then passed to the Continental Army.

In the Spying Business

One thing is certain; the enemy had
notice of our coming.

British officer after his defeat at Whitemarsh

On December 8, 1777, Lydia Darragh was summoned to British head-quarters in Philadelphia. Thin and pale, she trembled slightly as she took a seat across the table from the officer who wanted to talk to her.

While Lydia concentrated on trying to calm herself, the officer began to speak. He told her that for weeks the British had planned to surprise General Washington's men who were camped at nearby White-marsh. The planning, however, had been for naught, for Washington's men were well prepared for the surprise, and the British ended up marching back to Philadelphia, he said, "like a parcel of damned fools."[1] Someone should pay for this humiliation, and the officer thought that it should be the spy who had betrayed the British.

The woman listening to this angry report was well known and respected in Philadelphia. Her first employment in the city was that of a mortician. Exactly when she began to prepare the dead for burial isn't clear, but it is likely that she began to do so shortly after she and her husband, both of whom were from Ireland, arrived in Philadelphia. She was definitely in business by December 1766, when her first advertisement appeared in the *Pennsylvania Gazette*:

> The subscriber, living in Second Street, at the corner of Taylor's Alley, opposite the Golden Fleece Tavern, takes this method of informing the Public that she intends to make Grave-Clothes and lay out the Dead in the Neatest Manner, and as she is informed a Person in this Business is much wanted in this City, she hopes, by her Care, to give Satisfaction to those who will be pleased to favour her with their Orders.
>
> Lydia Darragh[2]

When this business floundered, Lydia switched her emphasis from the dead to the living, becoming a nurse and midwife. By the time the British occupied Philadelphia, she was well established. She was also the mother of nine children, five of whom survived childhood. And she was a spy.

Lydia had taken a number of risks while gathering information for the Patriots, but her latest risk was also her greatest, and for days she had feared the very meeting she was now enduring at headquarters. She had the perfect opportunity to hear and then pass on the information that ruined the British army's surprise attack, and British officers were well aware of this fact.

The Darraghs, who lived across the street from the Golden Fleece Tavern, British headquarters, had been forced to give up a room in their home so that officers could hold planning sessions there. In order to make room for the meetings, the Darraghs sent away their two youngest children, placing them with relatives just outside the city. In exchange, the British gave the Darraghs a pass, which, when presented to one of the many sentries posted all around the city, enabled the Darraghs to leave Philadelphia and visit their children whenever they wished to do so.

The British believed that they were quite safe in holding meetings in the Darragh home because the Darraghs were Quakers, a religious group that tried to remain neutral throughout the conflict. Therefore, it was assumed that family members would have little interest in anything that was said during any conference.

The officers, however, had misjudged this Quaker family. The Darraghs had quietly, but wholeheartedly, backed the Revolution from the beginning. In fact, the family's oldest son, Charles, had joined the Continental Army, and Lydia, long before the officers began to meet in her home, had routinely spied on British headquarters, noting who was coming and going.

Once meetings began to be held in her home, Lydia made the most of the opportunity, listening at the door to try to pick up any information that would be of use to the Patriots. She told what she had overheard to her husband, who wrote the information—in shorthand—on tiny slips of paper. These slips were wrapped around button forms, covered with cloth, and sewn onto fourteen-year-old John Darragh's jacket. John then took the family's pass, slipped on his jacket, and took the messages to his brother Charles, who was stationed at Whitemarsh.

On the night of December 2, 1777, British officers met in the Darragh home to complete plans for their attack on Whitemarsh on December 5. As usual, Lydia was listening in the next room. Unlike other information she had passed on, which could have come from several sources other than the Darragh household, Lydia assumed that the details of this highly secret assault would be discussed only in the safety of British headquarters or in her home. This meant that sending on the information would most likely alert the British to the family's espionage activities, putting all the Darraghs' lives in jeopardy. On the other hand, she knew that she had to warn General Washington. She spent all of December 3 trying to devise a plan that would protect her family and help the Continental Army.

Lydia finally decided to risk only her own life. She did not give the information to her husband, nor did she ask John to deliver the message.

Instead, on December 4, she took the pass and, using the pretext that she needed flour from a mill outside the city, she began the long walk to Washington's camp. About 6 miles (10 kilometers) north of Philadelphia, she ran into one of Washington's scouts—a young man whom she recognized—and she told him about the British plan. Lydia then turned around and walked back to the city, picking up a sack of flour along the way. When she returned home, she anxiously awaited the outcome of the battle and what lay in store for her.

Although others had also somehow managed to learn about the assault, Lydia's information, as she was well aware, was unique. She was able to provide details that made it possible for Washington to be fully prepared even though the British had several clever tricks to throw the Continentals off guard. Because the enemy was prepared for every British ploy, the British knew that they had been spied upon. Yet, incredible as it may seem, they did not suspect Lydia. When the officer finished his summary of the British defeat and began to question her, he simply asked her whether or not she might have had guests in the house who had overheard the meeting. Needless to say, Lydia was greatly relieved when she realized that she was not under suspicion.

Lydia was only one of many female volunteers who at some time during the war took it upon themselves to spy or carry messages for the Continental Army. How many actually participated is not known, for in many cases these women, who did not identify themselves, simply walked into an army camp and delivered the information they had. As a result, few are mentioned by name in official records, although numerous references are made to women delivering messages.

Women were also included in professional spy rings. Washington asked Major Benjamin Tallmadge, a close friend of the spy Nathan Hale (who had been hanged for espionage) to begin his own spy ring. Tallmadge, assisted by Robert Townsend, sought out people he knew well, including Anna Strong, Sally Townsend, who was Robert's sister, and a woman now known only as Agent 355.

*The home of the Darragh family, Loxley House,
was across the street from the Golden Fleece
Tavern, British headquarters in Philadelphia.*

Anna Strong's job was to inform Patriots in the New York area that information had arrived and then tell them where they could pick up the messages. Anna would know that a message had arrived when she received a midnight signal by lantern light from a nearby bay. The next morning she would hang a black petticoat on her clothesline, followed by at least one white handkerchief. The spy ring had listed every inlet in the area and then assigned each one a number; one hanky on the clothesline meant that a messenger was waiting in the first inlet on the list, and two hankies meant that the message could be picked up in the second inlet, and so on.

Sally Townsend assisted this ring by gathering information. Her father ran a boardinghouse near New York City, where she lived and worked. Several of the Townsends' boarders were British officers, including Lieutenant Colonel Simcoe, who supposedly was in love with Sally. On one occasion she overheard Simcoe and a visitor, known then as

John Anderson, talk about West Point, where the Patriots had stored large quantities of ammunition. On another occasion, Sally spotted John picking up a message from a little-used cupboard in the kitchen.

Shortly after, Anderson was stopped by two men thought to be thieves, who, after finding some strange papers in Anderson's boots, decided to take him to Patriot authorities. Anderson turned out to be Major John André, one of the most important British spies in the colonies. The papers that André carried, plus other information that the spy ring had gathered, proved that Benedict Arnold, a Patriot officer who was in command at West Point, was about to turn over his post to the British in exchange for a large sum of money. Once this plot was exposed, Arnold fled for his life. Although he was unable to turn over the post, he was able to give the British important information about Patriot troops and spies. Not too long after, André was hanged for his part in the scheme.

Like Sally Townsend, Agent 355 also gathered information; unlike Sally, this agent died because of her espionage activities. This mysterious woman, who was Robert Townsend's mistress, was arrested shortly after Benedict Arnold fled to the British lines. It is quite possible that Arnold warned the British about her. She was put aboard the infamous prison ship *Jersey*, which was filthy, overcrowded, and contaminated by disease. She died there, shortly after giving birth to Townsend's son.

――――

Some colonial women spied for the British. Most worked as volunteers, although some also became part of professional spy rings.

Rebecca Shoemaker, the wife of the Loyalist mayor of Philadelphia, gathered bits and pieces of information and passed them on in personal letters. She first came under suspicion in Philadelphia after the British had abandoned the city in June 1778. It wasn't until almost a year later, when she applied to the city council for permission to go to British-held New York, however, that she was investigated and her home was searched.

Suspicions about spying became secondary when one of the council members read Shoemaker's journal. Enraged by its contents, he told the council, "Mrs. Shoemaker, wife of Samuel Shoemaker, has . . . assisted prisoners [held by the patriots] and others, enemies to this government and to the United States, to pass [secretly] to New York."[3] The council then decided that Rebecca ought to join these enemies, and it gave her a pass enabling her to leave the city with the understanding that she could not return to Philadelphia without the council's permission, which in all likelihood would never be granted.

Another volunteer, Lorenda Holmes, gathered information and carried messages in the New York area. When she was caught, the Patriots, after rejoicing that they "have got the Damned Tory, the penny Post, at last,"[4] let her go, warning her that she would be severely punished if she was caught again.

Holmes continued to carry messages, though, and she took on another very dangerous task: helping Loyalists who wanted to join the British Army get through Patriot lines. She was caught again, and this time, in large part because she was actively helping the British Army increase its numbers, the Patriots decided to inflict the severe punishment they had promised. According to a statement she made after the incident, her captors told her to remove her shoes. A soldier then took, she said, "a shovel of Wood Coals from the fire and by mere force held [my] right foot upon the Coals until he had burnt it in a most shocking manner."[5]

Holmes was not the only Loyalist who spied for the British. Although records show that many women volunteered their services, only a few have been named: Elizabeth Henry; Elizabeth Gray, who was caught and imprisoned; Margaret Hutchinson, who routinely spied on Valley Forge; and Ann Bates, the most notorious of them all.

Ann Bates had been a teacher in Philadelphia before the war began. When she agreed to spy for the British, sometime in early 1778, she posed as a peddler, selling thread, needles, knives, and utensils to

Patience Lovell Wright (1725–1786)
Patriot Spy in London

Patience Lovell Wright was a successful artist who specialized in creating wax figures of famous people, one of the first women in the colonies to do so. Although Patience had received little formal education and what she knew about art was mostly self-taught, she was very skilled, and her work quickly became popular. By 1770, she had created enough wax models to make an impressive traveling show, which she took to New York and Charleston.

In 1772 she decided to continue her work in England. Benjamin Franklin, a friend of Patience's, was then living in London, and he introduced her to many wealthy and politically important people in the city. As she made wax figures of these people, she supposedly kept her clients entertained with witty conversation and tales of scandalous behavior committed by well-known aristocrats. She delighted in shocking people, and she actually addressed the king and queen, who agreed to pose for her, simply as "George" and "Charlotte."

Patience was a devoted Patriot, and when the war began she immediately began to work for the Continental Army. She easily picked up information not only from her clients but also from women with whom she socialized often. How she got her information to the colonies is not certain; legend has it that she hid messages inside some of her wax models, which she sent to the colonies for display. In any case, she was never suspected.

Patience thrived on danger. Toward the end of the Revolution, she became deeply involved in a plot to overthrow the king. Without financial backing, the plotters were forced to abandon their plan. Patience consoled herself by recognizing the part she had played in the American Revolution as one of the Patriots' most colorful spies.

This strange etching of Patience Lovell Wright appeared in a London magazine in 1775. She appears to be holding one of her wax figures—perhaps this reflects her reputation as a colorful and somewhat eccentric character.

Washington's camp followers. After she made a few sales in one camp, she moved on to the next, "by which means," she wrote later, "I had the Opportunity of going through their whole Army [noticing] at the same time the strength and situation of each Brigade, and the Number of Cannon with their Situation and Weight of Ball each Cannon was Charged with."[6] Not only could she count cannons, she could even identify the specific make of the guns. Ann had often watched her husband repair field pieces for the British, and this experience had made her very knowledgeable about weapons.

In addition to counting men and guns, Ann was given the names of several Loyalist sympathizers who were in the Continental Army, whom she was to contact when she reached their camps to collect their reports. She carried a token to show to each soldier to prove that she was a British spy, but what the token was remains a mystery to this day. Whatever it was, it never aroused suspicion; all British spies carried one, and yet whenever a spy was caught and searched, the token was overlooked.

By late summer 1778, she had become an incredibly valuable spy, and she was not unaware of her importance. She wrote about one of her accomplishments afterward, bragging that her information had saved a whole British garrison on Rhode Island. "My timly information was the blessed means of saving rowd island Garison with all the troops and stores who must otherwise [have] falen a pray to their Enemies."[7]

Ann took orders from General Duncan Drummond and John André, and she performed a number of tasks for them. Besides spying, she helped a British agent, a woman who has never been identified on record, cross Patriot lines and make the first contact with Benedict Arnold. Bates also briefed British and Loyalist spies and gave them a list of safe houses in their area where they could seek shelter from the Patriots.

But even though Ann was very skilled at what she did, her job was not without serious risk. By 1780 she was ready to leave the spying business. Her nerves were frazzled by the constant stress and danger, and Patriot counterintelligence agents were actively looking for her.

In addition, a number of safe houses were no longer safe. When the British captured Charleston, South Carolina, on May 12, Ann requested and received permission to join her husband there (where he was busy repairing guns), ending her spying career.

Even though female spies supplied very valuable information, they were often regarded more as a nuisance than a threat when caught, explaining, in part, why when they were caught they were never punished as severely as were Hale and André, who were hanged. Long after women like Lydia Darragh and Ann Bates delivered their information, generals still believed that women working for the other side really were not able to understand military matters—an attitude that only made it easier for women to spy.

In the Political Arena

Female opinions are of no consequence
in public matters.

from *Pennsylvania Packet*, a colonial newspaper

On October 25, 1774, fifty-one women in Edenton, North Carolina, performed a remarkable feat: They signed a proclamation that announced to the world that they had a duty to become involved in political issues that affected the colonies. Until then, colonial women had only joined spinning bees or boycotts when asked to do so; now the Edenton women intended to discuss issues and decide for themselves what actions to take. This proclamation, written by Penelope Barker, would get little attention in the world of today. But Barker's announcement was the first of its kind in American history, and because it was generally believed then that it was unladylike—even unnatural—for women to be interested in public matters, her proclamation got quite a reaction, especially in England.

Two articles and a cartoon about the Edenton women appeared in London newspapers. Readers of the articles wondered what kind of women would sign such a proclamation.

Penelope Barker, the author of the Edenton proclamation, was used to getting her own way. Even her husband could not persuade her to stay out of political matters.

The laughter that Philip Dawe's famous cartoon of the "Edenton Tea Party" first elicited quickly turned to anger as the British realized it interpreted the Edenton women's proclamation as vile and disrespectful.

At first glance, the cartoon caused laughter. This now-famous illustration portrayed the Edenton women as ugly hussies, which amused British subscribers. But the cartoon also featured a dog, a symbol for the women, urinating on a tea chest. As the cartoonist had hoped they would, readers saw the dog's activity as a sign of how little the women thought of British tea, which they had decided to boycott, as well as how little they thought of Britain, represented by the tea chest. After studying the cartoon and thinking about its message, readers concluded that the proclamation was not a laughing matter. Britain, they now believed, had been insulted by Barker and her followers, and readers were enraged.

The Edenton proclamation received two very different reactions in the colonies. When the women decided to back the boycott against British goods, Loyalists joined the British in condemning Barker's announcement. Patriots, on the other hand, needing all the support they could get, endorsed the women's proclamation. These men looked upon female involvement in public affairs as a temporary thing, and they assumed that once the crisis between Britain and the colonies was resolved, real ladies would once again refrain from showing any interest in politics.

Even though the Edenton women were the first to announce their intentions, they were not the only colonial women who wanted to have a voice in the historic events unfolding all around them. This desire was fueled by several things. First, as tensions increased between Great Britain and the colonies in the late 1760s and early 1770s, many colonial men passionately debated the pros and cons of the legislation passed by Parliament, and colonial women overheard some of these debates. As a result, although women were not supposed to be interested in such matters, they found it impossible to remain aloof. Two women summed up their predicament when one pointed out, "Nothing else is talked of," and the other wondered how women could avoid becoming interested in "the most animating Subject . . . one that Concerns us all."[1]

The desire to become involved in political matters was further fueled when colonial women were asked to participate in the boycotting of British goods. The effectiveness of the boycotts proved to women that they could play an important part in the dramatic conflict between the colonies and Great Britain, and the applause they received for their supporting roles greatly reinforced their newly acquired belief that political issues were very interesting matters.

In addition, as more and more arguments for independence were made by colonial leaders, women—including slaves—began to talk about freedom not only for their homeland but for themselves as well. They cast aside old roles they had been expected to play and challenged the old laws that limited what they could do; this eventually enabled many young women, wives, mothers, and grandmothers to participate in the Revolution.

Even though Patriot women began to see themselves in a different light, most who wanted to participate in public matters proceeded cautiously. Eliza Wilkinson, for example, asked only for the right to think for herself. She told a friend, "The men say we have no business with [politics], it is not in our sphere! I won't have it thought that because we are the weaker sex as to bodily strength, my dear, we are capable of nothing more than minding the dairy and visiting the poultry-house. . . . They won't even allow us the liberty of thought, and that is all I want."[2]

Mercy Otis Warren also proceeded cautiously, even though she was actually encouraged by Patriot leaders to take a part in the war effort. One of thirteen children of a wealthy family in Barnstable, Massachusetts, Mercy Otis was unusually well educated for that era. She attended a school for exceptional students with her brothers, and her parents encouraged her to study as much as possible when they realized that she was very intelligent.

Although many colonial women heard verbal attacks on British laws and King George just before the war started, Mercy was surrounded by talk of revolution long before it became popular. Mercy's husband, James Warren, was a dedicated Patriot, and her brother, James Otis, with whom she was especially close, was a Patriot firebrand who had for years roused crowds with his passionate statements against Great Britain.

Mercy showed great talent as a writer, and when she decided to use her pen as a weapon, she wrote plays that made fun of the British and needled the Loyalists, whom she detested. She named the Loyalists "Sir Spendall," "Judge Meagre," and "Hum Humbug," all of whom were surrounded by "hungry harpies" and "unprincipled danglers."

During the colonial period, plays were hardly ever performed on stage; instead, they were read much as we read stories today. Since many were published in newspapers or pamphlets, as were Mercy's plays, dramas could be enjoyed by many people, not just those close to a theater. This also meant that a play's message could reach many citizens.

Although Mercy Warren believed strongly in the message of her dramas, she published her works anonymously for two reasons: She feared punishment by the authorities, especially before the Revolution began, and she thought that writing plays about political issues was outside the realm of what a proper lady should do. She wrestled with this belief, often seeking reassurance from friends and family members.

Because she published her plays anonymously, historians have debated whether or not Mercy wrote all five dramas now credited to her: *The Adulateur* (1772), *The Defeat* (1773), *The Group* (1775), *The Blockheads* (1776), and *The Motley Assembly* (1779). The first three plays credited to her are significantly different from the last two; *The Blockheads* and *The Motley Assembly* contain extremely vulgar language. Even though Mercy wanted to make the British characters as repulsive as possible, some historians think it highly unlikely that she would have gone so far as to use an abundance of four-letter words.

Another writer who supported the Patriot cause was Phillis Wheatley. Phillis was a slave who was brought to the colonies from Africa in 1761 when she was about seven years old. Shortly after arriving, she was purchased by John and Susanna Wheatley of Boston, Massachusetts. The Wheatleys soon realized that Phillis was extremely bright, and they provided her with the best education possible. An exceptional student with a great talent for writing, she published her first poem when she was about seventeen years old.

Wheatley was given more freedom than most slaves, and this enabled her to worship at a church of her own choice. She attended the Old South Meeting House, which was the site of numerous Patriot meetings as well as of memorial services to honor the colonists who died in an event now known as the Boston Massacre. This massacre was the result of a clash between ten British soldiers and sixty angry colonists on March 5, 1770. Three colonists were killed outright by British soldiers, and two more died later from wounds they received in the struggle. Patriots often used this event to whip up support for their cause, and they held memorial services in the Old South Meeting House each year to commemorate the Revolution's first martyrs. Wheatley's biographers believe that her membership at the Old South Meeting House encouraged her to become a Patriot supporter in spite of the fact that her owners were staunch Loyalists.

Phillis made her support for the Patriots very clear in her poetry. One of her first poems about the Revolution was titled "On the Affray in King Street, on the Evening of the 5th of March." This poem honored the first person to be killed in the Boston Massacre, Crispus Attucks, an African-American man.

By 1772, Wheatley had enough poems about freedom and the Patriot cause to fill a book. However, she could not find a publisher who would take her work—not because of her political beliefs, but because of her sex and race.

Shortly after, one of Wheatley's poems came to the attention of Selina Hastings, a wealthy countess in England, and in 1773, Hastings offered to finance a book of Phillis's poetry. Wheatley accepted Hastings's offer, deciding to eliminate all poems about political issues from the

Offered many more opportunities than most African Americans in colonial times, Phillis Wheatley made the most of her education by studying history, geography, astronomy, and the Latin classics.

book to avoid creating a ruckus. Instead, she included poems on more traditional topics such as beauty and inspiration. If she had published her entire collection of poems, she would have been the first author, white or black, male or female, of a book of Revolutionary War poems.

Abigail Smith Adams, like Wheatley, was also interested in political issues. Abigail was the daughter of a Congregational minister and, through her mother, a member of one of the most elite families in New England, the Quincys.

Reverend William Smith taught his daughter how to read and write, and Abigail took it from there. She eagerly read numerous books on her own, selecting whatever interested her in her father's extensive library in their home in Weymouth, Massachusetts. When she couldn't find the information she wanted in this library, she borrowed books from her aunt's collection in nearby Boston. In addition, she often visited her grandfather, a leading political figure in Massachusetts, who allowed her to remain in the drawing room when local officials called on him. The men's conversations created a keen interest in politics in Abigail at a very early age. As a result of her serious efforts to learn as much as she could, Abigail acquired a remarkable education. Her husband, John Adams, considered her to be one of the brightest—and sauciest—women he ever met.

Abigail's husband was a lawyer and a member of both the First and Second Continental Congresses. He was instrumental in persuading the Second Congress to declare independence from Britain in 1776.

Because of John's involvement, Abigail was well versed on the Patriot cause, and three months before independence was declared, she anticipated how Congress would vote. Abigail saw a break with Great Britain as a wonderful opportunity for colonial women to gain rights that previously had been denied them by British law, and she even threatened to take political action if her requests were not met. In a letter dated March 31, 1776, she told her husband, who would help found a new government, to remember the ladies when making new laws. "Do not put such unlimited power into the hands of the husbands. Remember, all men would be tyrants if they could. If particular care and attention is not paid to the ladies, we are determined to [start] a rebellion, and will not hold ourselves bound by any laws in which we have no voice or representation."[3]

On April 14, 1776, John Adams responded to his wife's letter. "As to your extraordinary . . . laws, I cannot but laugh. We have been told that our struggle has loosened the bonds of government everywhere; that children and apprentices were disobedient; that schools and colleges were grown turbulent; that . . . [slaves] grew insolent to their masters. But your letter was the first intimation that [women], more numerous and powerful than all the rest, were grown discontented."[4] Needless to say, Abigail was more than a little miffed by her husband's dismissal of what she considered to be a very serious cause.

While Abigail usually shared her political views only with her husband and close friends, female publishers attempted to share their ideas and information with as many people as possible. During the war, at least six women published newspapers: Clementina Rind, Margaret Draper, Ann Catharine Green, Elizabeth Timothy, Mary Crouch, and Mary Katherine Goddard. All except Goddard became involved in publishing through their husbands, and all faced intense pressure during the war when the Patriots and Loyalists wanted only their side of an issue published.

Mary Katherine Goddard was the most successful female publisher during the Revolution. She became involved in newspaper publishing shortly after her father died. Her mother and brother William, who had been a printer's apprentice, started a paper, the *Providence Gazette*, in Rhode Island in 1762. When this paper failed, William somehow found the money to start another journal in Philadelphia. Mary Katherine and her mother joined him, eventually performing most of the work. William, who could never seem to settle down in one place for long, left Philadelphia within a few years to buy a printing shop in Baltimore. When her mother died, Mary Katherine once again joined her brother, and she began to publish the *Maryland Journal* on February 17, 1774. She also printed almanacs and pamphlets as well as special orders for customers.

During the war, Goddard had a difficult time finding supplies, especially the proper paper. Sometimes the *Journal* had to be printed on small sheets of paper, but Mary Katherine managed to put out a paper throughout the entire war, a feat that few publishers could match. Goddard's reporting helped keep Patriot readers up to date on the latest events of the war, often replacing rumors with facts, a major contribution to the cause.

It was Mary Katherine's professionalism that gained her the attention of many prominent patriots. When the Second Continental Congress needed to have copies of the Declaration of Independence printed so that it could be distributed to state legislatures, Patriot leaders turned

Abigail Adams recognized her opportunity and duty as wife of Continental Congress member John Adams to speak on behalf of women and their place in the proposed new government.

to Goddard. Early in 1777 she produced the first copies in the colonies that included the names of all the signers.

―――

Loyalist women also entered the political arena of the Revolution, but they faced several problems that Patriot women did not encounter. First, Loyalist women were expected to accept all of Britain's laws and social codes, including those that put limits on what women could do. In British eyes, it was neither acceptable nor desirable for women to publicly demonstrate their support for Great Britain.

In addition, Loyalists had difficulty expressing themselves because they were never as well organized as the Patriots, nor, remarkable as it may seem, did they band together for protection. This made supporting the British in any Patriot-held territory a dangerous thing to do. Known British sympathizers were tarred and feathered, forced to sit on blocks of ice until their buttocks froze to cool their ardor for Britain, and stripped naked in public to humiliate them. Sometimes Loyalists were repeatedly harassed in an attempt to drive them out of the area. Anna Rawle, the daughter of the Loyalist spy Rebecca Shoemaker, was often terrorized by Patriot supporters, who insisted on checking her rooms, rummaging through drawers and closets and trunks trying to find guns. Understandably, it took only a few violent incidents to silence many Loyalists, and as the Patriots took more territory, there were fewer safe places in which the king's supporters could voice their opinions.

As a result, most Loyalists, especially women, chose to keep their thoughts to themselves, expressing them only to close friends who were also Loyalists or in letters to friends in England. One of the most prolific letter writers of the revolution was Ann Hulton. She had little respect for the Patriots, whom she considered to be not much more than bandits, and she made this clear in one of her first letters of the Revolution:

> In [the British] army are many [soldiers] of noble family
> . . . and it grieves one that . . . brave British soldiers should fall

by the hands of such despicable wretches as compose the banditti of this country, among whom there is not one that has the least pretension to be called a gentleman. They are a most rude, depraved, degenerate race, and it is a mortification of [Loyalists] that they speak English and can trace themselves from that stock.[5]

Letter writing was not enough for some female Loyalists, though, and they chose to take a more active—and more dangerous—role. Margaret Draper, for example, published a paper for the Loyalists, the *Boston Newsletter*, which she inherited from her husband. Like Mary Katherine Goddard, Draper also printed materials for customers. One of her most important customers was the royal governor of Massachusetts.

Margaret was regularly attacked by Patriots in rival newspapers. She was accused of telling lies and having an evil heart as well as betraying her country. When she published a series of articles meant to encourage readers to support the British, Patriots were enraged. John Adams, using a pen name, responded in a paper that backed the Patriots, attacking each argument, trying to undermine any support the *Newsletter* might have achieved.

Draper continued her work until the British were forced to evacuate Boston on March 17, 1776. Once her protectors left, Margaret had little choice but to flee, and she moved to Canada shortly after. Her paper was the last to support the British cause in the colonies.

One of the most ardent supporters of the British, Mary Brant, lived on the frontier in what is now western New York State. Mary was a member of the Iroquois Confederacy, which consisted of the Seneca, Cayuga, Mohawk, Oneida, Onondaga, and Tuscarora Indian tribes. She was also the wife of the late Sir William Johnson, Britain's superintendent for Indian Affairs, who died in 1774.

Shortly before the Revolution began, both the colonists and the British approached the Iroquois Confederacy to see what position it would take in the coming war. The confederacy had backed the British in the French and Indian War (1754–1763), and because the Iroquois suffered many casualties during that conflict, tribal leaders decided that it was in the best interests of the Indians to stay out of a war that they believed would have little effect upon them no matter who won. At first, both the British and the Patriots were relieved by this decision.

By late 1776, though, British generals, who now realized that the colonists were not going to be easy to defeat, changed their position: They decided that it was in their best interest to persuade the Iroquois to join them. Not only could the Iroquois supply two thousand warriors, but they could attack settlers on the frontier and force the colonists to fight on two fronts at once, dividing their already understaffed army, weakening it to such a point that the British could more easily win the war.

This decision by military leaders was met with harsh criticism in Parliament. Several representatives were afraid that the Indians, who had a very different approach to warfare, would prove to be a liability, not an asset. These representatives argued that Iroquois raids could turn even more colonists against the British and cause an international outcry when the Indians took captives to torture or enslave or, worse yet, murdered and scalped women and children as they had done in the past.

Nevertheless, agents from the British Army approached the Iroquois in September 1776. Mary Brant then became involved in the Iroquois' decision.

Unlike colonial women, Iroquois women had long had a voice in tribal affairs. In fact, they elected the men who represented them at confederacy meetings. Mary was one of the most influential women in the confederation. According to one eyewitness, "one word from her goes farther with [the warriors] than a thousand from any white man without exception."[6] Because she deeply believed that it was in the best interest of her people to support the British, who now vowed to stop the colonists from moving westward onto Indian lands if Britain won the war, Mary abandoned neutrality and threw her support to the British.

Ann Lee (1736–1784)

One of the most outspoken opponents of the Revolution was Ann Lee. Born in England, Lee immigrated to the colonies in 1774, along with nine followers, to spread her religious beliefs. According to Lee, who had had several religious visions, Jesus Christ, whom many Christians believed would come to Earth a second time, had now arrived. He did not appear as a man, though, as most people thought would happen; instead he came as a woman—Ann Lee herself.

Ann and her followers purchased property near Albany, New York, where they started the Church of Christ's Second Coming. Lee's religious ideas appealed to many, and she quickly built an impressive following in the New England area. Because many religious meetings involved movements of the body that resembled shaking, Lee's followers became known as Shakers.

When the Revolution started in 1775, Lee did not hesitate to express her opinions on public issues. She condemned the Patriots, calling them un-Christian for fighting in a revolution. Her verbal assaults, which increased over the years, understandably upset the Patriots.

By 1780 she had convinced many colonists that the war was a sinful undertaking. Local militias then believed that they had to silence her; they did so by putting her in jail.

But as soon as Lee was released, she resumed her attacks. Enraged militiamen then stormed her home, knocked her down, dragged her outside, and threw her into a sleigh. She was taken to a nearby farm where she was stripped to determine whether or not she really was a woman. It was assumed that this frightful treatment would silence her. However, much to the chagrin of her captors, she resumed her anti-Patriot stance as soon as she was released, and she remained committed to this position throughout the war.

Although she failed to convince the leaders of the Tuscaroras and Onei-das, the other four tribes followed her advice. Led by Mary's brother, Joseph Brant, these Indians wreaked havoc on the frontier, and they proved to be very valuable allies for the British—for a while.

On July 27, 1777, when Iroquois scouts seized two women, Mrs. Sarah McNeil and Jane McCrea, at Mrs. McNeil's home on the frontier, some of Parliament's worst fears came true. Ironically, McNeil and Mc-Crea, who was engaged to a Loyalist officer stationed nearby, were Loyalists.

Although both women tried to make their position known as the scouts dragged them out of the house and into the nearby woods, the Indians paid no attention to what was being said. They insisted on following the orders they had been given at all costs: They were supposed to create havoc on the frontier so that the colonists would have to send troops. McCrea, who was young, beautiful, and the devout daughter of a clergyman, was murdered and scalped when the scouts got into a fight over what should be done with her, and her bleeding, mangled body was left for wild animals to devour.

When word of this event reached the Patriots, it created the very uproar the warriors had wanted to achieve, but it hurt the British cause more than it helped it.

Although the warriors' terrible attack—and many others like it—eventually did force the colonists to send troops to the frontier, McCrea's death made the colonists more determined than ever to beat the British and their allies. Also, army recruiters used McCrea's death to bolster their cause and enlist more soldiers. McCrea's death, they argued, was proof that the British and their allies were dastardly villains who murdered women, even Loyalist women. What, they wondered aloud, would such barbarians do to their enemies? In addition, the publicity that surrounded McCrea's death made it even more dangerous for Loyalists to admit their support for the king, let alone take action to support him. For most, the only way they could be safe was to be quiet.

The SENTIMENTS of an
AMERICAN WOMAN.

ON the commencement of actual war, the Women of America manifested a firm resolution to contribute as much as could depend on them, to the deliverance of their country. Animated by the purest patriotism, they are sensible of sorrow at this day, in not offering more than barren wishes for the success of so glorious a Revolution. They aspire to render themselves more really useful; and this sentiment is universal from the north to the south of the Thirteen United States. Our ambition is kindled by the fame of those heroines of antiquity, who have rendered their sex illustrious, and have proved to the universe, that, if the weakness of our Constitution, if opinion and manners did not forbid us to march to glory by the same paths as the Men, we should at least equal, and sometimes surpass them in our love for the public good. I glory in all that which my sex has done great and commendable. I call to mind with enthusiasm and with admiration, all those acts of courage, of constancy and patriotism, which history has transmitted to us: The people favoured by Heaven, preserved from destruction by the virtues, the zeal and the resolution of Deborah, of Judith, of Esther! The fortitude of the mother of the Macchabees, in giving up her sons to die before her eyes: Rome saved from the fury of a victorious enemy by the efforts of Volumnia, and other Roman Ladies: So many famous sieges where the Women have been seen forgetting the weakness of their sex, building new walls, digging trenches with their feeble hands, furnishing arms to their defenders, they themselves darting the missile weapons on the enemy, resigning the ornaments of their apparel, and their fortune, to fill the public treasury, and to hasten the deliverance of their country; burying themselves under its ruins; throwing themselves into the flames rather than submit to the disgrace of humiliation before a proud enemy.

Born for liberty, disdaining to bear the irons of a tyrannic Government, we associate ourselves to the grandeur of those Sovereigns, cherished and revered, who have held with so much splendour the scepter of the greatest States, The Batildas, the Elizabeths, the Maries, the Catharines, who have extended the empire of liberty, and contented to reign by sweetness and justice, have broken the chains of slavery, forged by tyrants in the times of ignorance and barbarity. The Spanish Women, do they not make, at this moment, the most patriotic sacrifices, to encrease the means of victory in the hands of their Sovereign. He is a friend to the French Nation. They are our allies. We call to mind, doubly interested, that it was a French Maid who kindled up amongst her fellow-citizens, the flame of patriotism buried under long misfortunes: It was the Maid of Orleans who drove from the kingdom of France the ancestors of those same British, whose odious yoke we have just shaken off; and whom it is necessary that we drive from this Continent.

But I must limit myself to the recollection of this small number of atchievements. Who knows if persons disposed to censure, and sometimes too severely with regard to us, may not disapprove our appearing acquainted even with the actions of which our sex boasts? We are at least certain, that he cannot be a good citizen who will not applaud our efforts for the relief of the armies which defend our lives, our possessions, our liberty? The situation of our soldiery has been represented to me; the evils inseparable from war, and the firm and generous spirit which has enabled them to support these. But it has been said, that they may apprehend, that, in the course of a long war, the view of their distresses may be lost, and their services be forgotten. Forgotten! never; I can answer in the name of all my sex. Brave Americans, your disinterestedness, your courage, and your constancy will always be dear to America, as long as she shall preserve her virtue.

We know that at a distance from the theatre of war, if we enjoy any tranquility, it is the fruit of your watchings, your labours, your dangers. If I live happy in the midst of my family; if my husband cultivates his field, and reaps his harvest in peace; if, surrounded with my children, I myself nourish the youngest, and press it to my bosom, without being affraid of seeing myself separated from it, by a ferocious enemy; if the house in which we dwell; if our barns, our orchards are safe at the present time from the hands of those incendiaries, it is to you that we owe it. And shall we hesitate to evidence to you our gratitude? Shall we hesitate to wear a cloathing more simple; hair dressed less elegant, while at the price of this small privation, we shall deserve your benedictions. Who, amongst us, will not renounce with the highest pleasure, those vain ornaments, when she shall consider that the valiant defenders of America will be able to draw some advantage from the money which she may have laid out in these; that they will be better defended from the rigours of the seasons, that after their painful toils, they will receive some extraordinary and unexpected relief; that these presents will perhaps be valued by them at a greater price, when they will have it in their power to say: *This is the offering of the Ladies.* The time is arrived to display the same sentiments which animated us at the beginning of the Revolution, when we renounced the use of teas, however agreeable to our taste, rather than receive them from our persecutors; when we made it appear to them that we placed former necessaries in the rank of superfluities, when our liberty was interested; when our republican and laborious hands spun the flax, prepared the linen intended for the use of our soldiers; when exiles and fugitives we supported with courage all the evils which are the concomitants of war. Let us not lose a moment; let us be engaged to offer the homage of our gratitude at the altar of military valour, and you, our brave deliverers, while mercenary slaves combat to cause you to share with them, the irons with which they are loaded, receive with a free hand our offering, the purest which can be presented to your virtue,

By An AMERICAN WOMAN.

Esther Reed's broadside, published
June 10, 1780, in Philadelphia.

In the Ladies Association

It must strike the enemy as with an apoplexy,
to be informed, that the women of America
are attentive to the wants of the Soldiery.

the *Pennsylvania Packet*, a colonial newspaper

On May 12, 1780, Charleston, South Carolina, was taken by the British. This was a bitter defeat for the Patriots, for they realized that the war, which was now five years old, was not about to end in the near future. Continental soldiers were not only disheartened but they suffered from the lack of clothing, ammunition, and weapons needed to fight a winning campaign. As if that wasn't bad enough, the army was in sore need of more soldiers to replace those who had served their enlisted time or were too exhausted to fight.

While Patriot leaders struggled to find sources from which they could borrow money so that supplies could be purchased abroad and more soldiers could be hired, patriot women looked about, trying to find some way to improve the army's morale. In Philadelphia, Esther Reed, who had moved from England to the colonies shortly after her marriage to Joseph Reed in 1770, decided to start a nationwide fund drive. She wanted to give a gift of money to each soldier. She hoped that such a gift would demonstrate to the soldiers the dedication of women to the Patriot cause and make them aware that their sacrifices were genuinely appreciated.

Reed's fund drive was the first of its kind in America, and because she was taking on a nontraditional role, she proceeded very carefully in order to lessen criticism. She began her campaign with the publication of a broadside, a large poster that explained why women should become involved in helping the Patriot army. First, she explained that what she proposed really was not new, and she backed her claim with examples of women in ancient history who had helped soldiers. Then Reed explained that while some men might object to women organizing a money-raising project under normal circumstances, these were not ordinary times. Besides, she said that she found it difficult to believe that any true Patriot would deny women the opportunity to help Washington's soldiers. She ended her broadside with a plea for money.

Shortly after Reed's plea appeared, thirty-six women met in Philadelphia to devise a plan for the group, now called the Association, to collect money from women all over the city. Reed hoped that this plan would be copied by women in other cities so that this drive would become a national campaign.

In order to give the fund status, wives of husbands with the highest social standing were asked to collect the money. These wives included Mary Morris, wife of the chief financier of the army, whose job it was to find enough money to run the Revolution; Sally McKean, wife of Pennsylvania's chief justice; and Sarah Bache, wife of a prominent businessman in Philadelphia and the daughter of Benjamin Franklin.

Even though Reed's group included some of the most socially prominent women in Philadelphia, Loyalist women regarded the fund drive as one of the most disgusting events they had ever witnessed. Women, especially wives, were not supposed to be concerned about financial matters and only the lowliest would ask strangers for money. What made the situation even more appalling in the Loyalists' eyes— besides the fact that the money was going to be used by their enemies— was the fact that Reed and her supporters were so bold. Anna Rawle, a Loyalist, described the shocking scene in a letter to her mother. Rawle said that the ladies actually arrived with ink pens in hand to record donations, and the women would not take no for an answer. "Of all absurdities," she added, "the Ladies going about for money exceeded everything. . . . People were obliged to give them something to get rid of them."[1]

Fund collectors tried to give every woman a chance to donate something to the drive, although collectors were known to pass by houses of staunch Loyalists like Anna Rawle. Volunteers believed that a large sum of money would not only boost the Patriots' spirits but it would prove that the colonists were not as divided as British leaders thought. In short, a successful drive could, as one fund-raiser said, "blast the hopes of the enemies of this country."[2]

Volunteers in Philadelphia raised more than $300,000 in Continental money. Even though this sum was in highly inflated dollars and worth only about $7,000 in gold, the drive was still a great success. Other Patriot women followed the example set by Reed's organization, and soon other Ladies Associations organized similar campaigns in at least seven other colonies.

Reed's original plan for providing soldiers with a gift of money ran into difficulty, though, from an unexpected quarter. When she approached General Washington with her idea, he vetoed it. While he greatly appreciated the women's wish to reward the soldiers for all their sacrifices, Washington was afraid that the men might use the money to purchase liquor, and this could cause serious problems among his soldiers. Washington asked instead that the women provide much-needed clothing. Although Reed was very disappointed at having to give what she considered to be a rather commonplace gift, she accepted

Determined to contribute any way they could, women organized campaigns to sew uniforms for troops, an outlet for their patriotism that was viewed as acceptable to society.

Washington's advice, and the women of Pennsylvania began making plans for the manufacture of linen shirts for the soldiers.

Esther Reed did not live to see her plans completed. Only two weeks after the volunteers purchased the material, Esther was struck down by dysentery, and she died within days, leaving behind five children, the oldest only nine years old.

Sarah Franklin Bache then assumed Reed's role. A room was set aside in her house, and volunteers came and went regularly until 2,200 shirts were ready for delivery. Each one was signed by the woman who made it, and the soldiers who received these shirts were grateful for the clothing and deeply touched by the sentiments that produced them.

Esther Reed's drive to help the soldiers was only one voluntary effort made by women during the war. Many women, such as Betsy Ross, made regimental banners around which soldiers could rally. Catherine Smith and Elizabeth Hager, whose husbands had taught them how to make and repair guns, volunteered their services to the Patriots. And some women formed circles called Daughters of Liberty, which had the purpose of knitting socks or weaving cloth for uniforms, feminine tasks that were quite acceptable and highly encouraged as well.

In fact, only a few months after the Revolution began, the *Pennsylvania Magazine* urged women to increase their output of fabric, a product that could no longer be purchased from Great Britain. The editor said, "While the men defend our borders . . . the women must not neglect what is proper in their sphere. . . . As we must furnish clothing for many thousands more than we have heretofore done, the Spinning Wheel requires their particular attention. . . . There are at least 600,000 females in these Thirteen Colonies, of an age [six and older] sufficient to spin."[3]

Women also held scrap drives to collect unused pewter dishes that could be melted down and made into bullets. When a lead statue of King George, which weighed more than two tons, was pulled down by Patriots in New York, a group of women helped to break the statue into small pieces, melt the lead, and pour the molten metal into bullet molds, producing more than 40,000 musket balls.

As in all the American wars to follow, women who wanted to supply soldiers during the Revolutionary War had to make significant sacrifices. This was especially true for women who were wives and mothers. Already burdened by many household chores, would-be suppliers had to find time for another task. They also had to assume another financial responsibility—and many had very limited incomes—or they had to turn to fund drives as Esther Reed did. And because there were few wartime industries where women could either volunteer their services or join the work force, almost all supplies to be donated were made in women's homes. Still, few complained about their lot.

———

Loyalist women had even fewer opportunities to supply their troops than they did to express themselves on public issues. This was due, in large part, to fear of reprisal. Loyalist women started circles and associations in response to Reed's Ladies Association and the numerous volunteer groups that called themselves Daughters of Liberty. However, Loyalist associations were small—one in Boston had only eight members—and if these groups achieved much, their accomplishments were not recorded. Instead, it appears that the women met more to keep up each other's spirits and to show their contempt for the Patriots' tea boycott by holding traditional tea parties, complete with delicate sandwiches and dainty pastries.

Although details are sketchy, one group of Loyalist women managed to purchase and outfit a ship to help the British cause. Privateers, as they were called, were privately owned ships whose crew members had written permission from the British government to attack and seize any colonial ship during the war. If the privateers were captured by Patriots, these letters protected the sailors by making them a semiofficial part of the British Navy. Therefore, in the event of capture, the sailors were supposed to be treated as if they were prisoners of war. On the other hand, if a privateer's crew without the necessary permission letter was caught looting an enemy ship, the crew could be tried for piracy, a criminal offense that could result in hanging. Privateer crews were allowed to sell the cargoes of ships they captured and divide the money among the sailors according to a prearranged formula. They also could keep the captured ships, outfit them for privateering, and put them to work. Sometimes a portion of the profits was to be given to the British government.

Privateering not only enriched the crews and their owners, it also helped the war effort. These ships harassed the Patriots and kept desperately needed products from reaching colonial ports. Privateers also prevented colonial articles meant for sale in Europe from reaching their destinations, limiting the colonists' income. The women's gift of a privateer, then, was a very valuable donation.

The practice of allowing privateers to join the war was not limited to the British, though; the colonies had at least 1,700 privateers at work at some point during the Revolution. Although the vast majority of the sailors were men, teenagers and women also joined the crews of privateers. These sailors became suppliers for the Revolution, for they seized ships, goods, arms, and munitions worth millions of dollars, and they provided General Washington with many of the tools he needed to win the war.

The Betsy Ross Story:
Fact or Fiction?

The story about Betsy Ross (1752–1836) making the first American flag was first told by her grandson, William Canby. According to Canby, Ross, who was a seamstress by trade, was asked by a congressional committee to make a flag for the new nation. When the committee, headed by George Washington, asked Ross to sew a flag that had six-pointed stars, she suggested using stars with five points instead, because they were so easy to make. This design greatly pleased the committee, and it quickly accepted her idea.

Canby's story appeared to be just what the public wanted to hear. The story was repeated in *Harper's Monthly*, a popular magazine, during the first centennial celebration of the United States. Looking for female heroines to highlight, other sources picked up on the story, and soon it became one of the most popular tales ever told. It has even been included in a number of history textbooks.

However, most historians doubt that Betsy Ross made the first flag. They point out that there are no written records to support Canby's claim. If the committee had ordered the flag, they argue, there should be a written request as well as a record of payment in Ross's accounts and in Congress's ledgers. Furthermore, no eyewitnesses came forward to verify the story.

The debate over the story of Betsy Ross highlights a major problem historians face when studying the past: trying to determine what is fact and what is fiction. There are numerous stories about women in the Revolution that were not told until many years after the war ended. These stories, such as the one about Emily Geiger, who carried an important message through enemy lines for the Patriots, have long been challenged by historians—and rightly so—for there's simply no proof to support them. As a result, some stories that were probably true have been dismissed as legend, and our history is poorer for their loss.

*Like Molly Pitcher, Betsy Ross is a figure familiar
to most Americans. Also like Molly Pitcher, some
dispute her role in the American Revolution.*

With their men away fighting for independence, women were left to safeguard their homes, farms, and other property. Faced with an advance of British troops, Catherine Schuyler decided to burn her cornfields rather than let them be looted by the enemy.

On the Home Front

The house this instant shakes with the
roar of cannon . . . no sleep for me tonight.

Abigail Adams, Patriot

Sixteen-year-old Sally Wister, bored and restless, spent most of the summer of 1777 staring down the long dirt road that led to the farmhouse in which she and her family had sought shelter. The Wisters recently had fled from nearby Philadelphia, as had many families, when they learned that the British were about to take the city. These civilians, hoping to avoid being caught up in bloody battles, had appealed to friends and relatives in nearby rural areas to house them for a while. The Wisters had been welcomed by the Foulke family, where they were given the run of half of the family's small farmhouse.

Sally longed for Philadelphia and her friends. To pass time until she could see them again, she started a journal that was addressed to her best friend, Debby Norris. Her journal clearly shows the overwhelming fear that many women faced during the war as armies struggled for control of the colonies:

This day [September 25, 1777]. . .Hobson Jones . . . said the British were at Skippack Road . . . and that a party of Hessians had actually turned into our lane. . . . The delicate, chicken-hearted Liddy and I were wretchedly scared. We could say nothing but "Oh! What shall we do? What will become of us?"

Well the fright went off. We saw no [troops]. O. Foulke came here in the evening and told us that General Washington had come down as far as the Trappe . . . so we expected to be in the midst of one army or t'other.

About twelve o'clock [September 26] . . . somebody came to me in a hurry, screaming "Sally, Sally, here are the light horse [brigade]!" This was by far the greatest fright I had endured; fear tacked wings to my feet [as I ran to the porch to see for myself]. It really was the light horse.[1]

Sally panicked at the arrival of soldiers for several reasons. First, there was a genuine fear for her and her family's physical safety. Although many officers in both armies tried to protect civilians, some failed to do so. As a result, colonists were attacked, and the most common attack against women was rape. In late 1776, for example, sixteen girls in Hopewell, New Jersey, were captured and dragged to a British camp, where they were held captive and raped. A thirteen-year-old girl in a nearby town was sexually assaulted by six soldiers, and in Newark, New Jersey, one colonist noted that groups of officers went "about the town by night, entering into houses and openly inquiring for women."[2]

How many rapes occurred is not known. Many women did not report sexual assaults because of the embarrassment and humiliation that rape victims faced in colonial society. Besides, it seldom paid to report the crime. If a brave victim did go to the authorities and the assailant was identified, arrested, and court-martialed, officials often did not regard rape as a serious crime, and therefore the punishment would be light.

Besides being assaulted, civilians also feared that their property would be taken or destroyed by soldiers. Stories about theft and destruction were common. Eliza Wilkinson's tale was typical. Her home in South Carolina was ransacked by a British soldier and several Loyalist supporters, who robbed her of clothes and jewelry. While she and her daughters watched them ransack her home, the thieves, according to Eliza, used "the most abusive language imaginable, while making as if to hew us to pieces with their swords. . . . I trembled so with terror, that I could not support myself [stand]."[3]

Besides fearing assault and theft, Sally Wister was frightened by the appearance of soldiers because she thought that her family might be forced to quarter, or house, them. There was little one could do in the face of powerful armed troops, and although both Continental and British officers were supposed to find people who were willing to take them in, some officers decided to save time by commandeering shelter.

How much space soldiers demanded varied. Sometimes homeowners were able to limit the area to only a room or two, as did the spy Lydia Darragh. On the other hand, an army's demands could be extreme. Rebecca Motte, a wealthy Patriot in Charleston, South Carolina, was forced to turn over her entire plantation home to British officers. She surrendered her home, but her anger was so great that she later told Patriots to burn her mansion to the ground in order to drive out the British, an order the Patriots followed. Legend has it that Rebecca actually gave the Patriots some arrows, which were to be set ablaze and then fired at the roof of her house. Later, the British told her to surrender some rooms in her town house in the city as well.

Quartering troops created a number of problems, as Sally was well aware. Besides the loss of privacy and being forced to share scarce rations, additional people meant additional chores for women who already had their hands full. Extra tasks were less burdensome when Patriot women were putting up Continental soldiers or Loyalist women were helping British troops, but just barely so.

Quartering troops could also result in property damage and constant disruptions. One Long Island woman who was forced to put up Hessian officers noted that the soldiers, who were fond of roaring fires, "take the fence rails to burn, so that the fields are all left open, and the cattle stray away and are often lost." When the soldiers received their pay, she added, "we have trying and grievous scenes to go through; fighting, brawls, drumming and fifing, and dancing the night long; card and dice playing, and every abomination going on under our very roofs."[4]

Putting up troops, even for a day, could be dangerous as well, as Mary Slocumb learned. Mary and her husband, Zeke, lived on a large plantation near the Neuse River in North Carolina. In the early autumn of 1781, Lieutenant Colonel Banastre Tarleton, an English officer who commanded Loyalists in the South, arrived at the Slocumbs' home. He wanted to encamp his troops for the night on their property. Mary was both repulsed and horrified to have to deal with Tarleton, who was known for his cruelty. Believing that she had little choice but to grant permission to his troops, she told Tarleton that the men could camp near the peach orchard.

Fortunately, Mary's husband, a member of the local militia, was away when the troops arrived. Mary knew that Tarleton's presence was a great threat to her husband's life, however, and she quickly devised a plan to warn Zeke. As soon as possible, Mary began to prepare food for the officers. Under the guise of needing something for the meal, she told the officers that she had to send a servant to a nearby plantation. On the way, this servant was supposed to find Mary's husband and warn him about the danger at home.

Unfortunately, Tarleton's scouts, sent out to secure the area, found Slocumb and several other Patriots before the servant did. A skirmish took place, and the Patriots, having killed about half of the scouts, went after those who had fled for cover. Zeke pursued one of the Loyalists right onto the Slocumb plantation in full view of Tarleton and Mary, both of whom had rushed outside when they heard gunshots. Another servant then shouted to Zeke to go away. Confused, Zeke looked around and saw Tarleton and Mary, who was pointing to the soldiers by the orchard. Before the enemy could mount, Zeke turned, spurred his horse, and shouted to the other Patriots to follow him. All managed to reach safety, although they ducked a fair amount of shot before getting away.

The arrival of troops and requests for quarters also alarmed women because the soldiers' presence meant that the war had literally come to their doorsteps. Sometimes the soldiers' arrival and stay was peaceful, or it might result only in brief clashes similar to the events on the Slocumb plantation. More often, especially if officers were seeking lodgings for a lengthy period of time, requests for shelter meant that a major battle was about to take place nearby.

In Sally Wister's case, the battle at Whitemarsh was in the making when Continental Army officers requested lodgings at the Foulke farmstead. These officers and their troops wanted to annoy the British in Philadelphia by hovering nearby, making the British believe that they might be attacked at any moment. The Continental soldiers, the majority of whom were encamped at Whitemarsh, were very successful. The British retaliated by planning a surprise attack to end the Continental threat once and for all.

When the British left Philadelphia—and spy Lydia Darragh anxiously awaited the outcome of the battle—Sally awaited the beginning of the fighting. On December 5, she wrote, "Oh, gracious Debby, I am all alive with fear. The English have come out to attack . . . our army. [The British] are on Chestnut Hill, our army three miles this side. What will become of us, only six miles distant. We are in hourly expectation of an engagement. I fear we shall be in the midst of it. Heaven defend us from so dreadful a sight."[5]

Sally Wister was spared the horrible sights of battle, for the British were unable to surprise the Patriots, and the major engagement they had planned never took place. And as Washington withdrew his troops to Valley Forge later that month, the threat to the Wisters lessened greatly.

Sally was not the only woman to feel the effects of the war on the home front. Many women, Patriot and Loyalist alike, were forced to house the enemy, and those women whose husbands were away were forced to defend the family's property, earn an income, and protect their families as well.

Patriot women on farms were constantly faced with the threat of losing animals and crops to the enemy. Loyalists had some unscrupulous characters in their midst, and more than a few turned to cattle rustling to supply the British troops with fresh meat, a treat for which British officers would gladly pay large sums. Crops in the field were also fair game. If women could not protect these, they often decided to destroy the crops if there was any chance that the enemy might get them. Catherine Schuyler, for example, burned her wheat fields in New York State to prevent the British from taking her grain.

While Patriot women struggled to protect their produce, many Loyalist women had to defend their property from confiscation by the Patriots in Patriot-held areas. Often these women tried to hold on to property by simply refusing to leave it, hoping that Patriot organizations would not evict a helpless woman from her home.

Grace Galloway was one of the first to try this strategy. After hiring a lawyer to fight her eviction, she entrenched herself in her home, preparing for a long struggle. Grace was married to Joseph Galloway, a famous Loyalist pamphleteer. When the British abandoned Philadelphia in 1778 and the Continental Army took control of the city, Mr. Galloway and other prominent Loyalists were ordered to surrender themselves to the Supreme Executive Council of Pennsylvania. If they failed to do so, the council said that it would seize their property and sell it to the highest bidder. When Galloway chose to flee to England rather than surrender, the council claimed the Galloway home, which Grace had inherited from her father. This house had been put in her husband's name after she married him. Grace insisted that she should not be punished for her husband's actions, but the Patriots would not back down, claiming that the house was not legally hers.

Mrs. Galloway soon found herself all alone, for Loyalist friends were afraid to take any action that might draw attention to themselves. Grace confined most of her observations about her struggle to keep her home to her journal. On July 21, she noted:

> About 2 o'clock they came. . . . They took an inventory of everything, even to broken china and empty bottles. . . . They told me that they must advertise the house. I told them they may do as they pleased, but 'till it was decided by a court, I would not go out unless by the force of a bayonet. . . . I sent three times for Lewis [her lawyer], but he would not come. I sent for Ben Chew [a friend]. He came but thought I talked too high to those men. . . . He tells me I can't stay in the house. Yet on my saying "Where should I go?" never offered to take me in. . . . Not one has offered me a house to shelter me. . . . Oh God, what shall I do?[6]

On August 10, a man who agreed to purchase the Galloway house from the council moved in. Grace then confined herself to one of the rooms in the house before giving up the fight and moving in with the Morris family, which finally came to her rescue.

Women also had to earn their family's income if their husbands were in the service, for a soldier's pay was often scant and usually late. The vast majority of colonists lived on farms, but raising crops had not been part of women's work. Therefore, few had been given any instruction on how to plant and harvest. As a result, at the beginning of the war, women repeatedly wrote to their husbands begging for advice. When many of these wives were given detailed instructions, they learned how to raise desperately needed foodstuffs not only for their families but for the war effort as well. As these women realized some success, their confidence grew, and they began to make decisions on their own. Women then began to refer to the farms, once thought to belong only to their husbands, as "our" farms, a major change in perception.

Not all women became successful farmers, though. Some begged their husbands to return so that their children would have enough to eat. This became such a serious problem that Washington ordered his guards to keep unknown women away from army camps, afraid that they had come to take their husbands home.

Other farm wives just barely got by. One man, many years after the war had ended, recalled his mother's heroic efforts to provide for her family:

> My father was in the army during the whole eight years of the Revolutionary War. . . . My mother had the sole charge of four little ones. Our house was a poor one, and far from neighbors. I have a keen remembrance of the terrible cold of some of those winters. The snow lay so deep and long that it was difficult to cut or draw fuel from the woods, or to get our corn to the mill, when we had any. My mother was the possessor of a coffee-mill. In that she ground wheat and made coarse bread, which we ate, and were thankful. . . . Many is the time that we [went] to bed with only a drink of water for our supper, in which a little molasses had been mingled. We patiently received it, for we knew our mother did as well for us as she could; and we hoped to have something better in the morning.
>
> When my father was permitted to come home, his pay was short, and he had not much to leave us. . . . Yet when he went, my mother ever bade him farewell with a cheerful face, and told him not to be anxious about his children, for she would watch over them night and day. . . . Sometimes we wondered that she did not mention the cold weather, or our short meals, or her hard work. . . . But she would not weaken his hands or sadden his heart, for she said a soldier's life was harder than all.[7]

Success at running a family business also depended a great deal upon how much husbands had taught their wives. Often women became overwhelmed with business details, and many widows who had been left with businesses sold out. This was not always a wise decision, for sometimes unscrupulous purchasers took advantage of these women.

In the South, where most of the fighting took place, women in charge of plantations faced problems unknown to most Northern women. Like Northern businesses, plantation owners had lost their main trading partner, Britain. Unlike Northern businesses, though, plantation owners could not find ready markets in the colonies for some of their crops, such as indigo. As a result, many Southerners lost their major source of income for many years. In addition, Patriot plantation owners also faced the possible loss of their slaves. On June 30, 1779, General Henry Clinton, who led British forces in the New York area and wanted to upset the home front, invited all slaves owned by Patriots to try to escape from their masters. If these slaves could reach British forces, they would be regarded as free men and women. An estimated 10,000 slaves took up Clinton's offer just in the Charleston, South Carolina–Savannah, Georgia area. A large number of these slaves were women with children, some of whom were then put to work in British camps.

Because of the unrest among slaves brought about by the constant talk of freedom in the colonies and Clinton's promise, Southern women feared not only losing their slaves but slave uprisings as well while their husbands were away. This was a very threatening situation to plantation mistresses, especially in colonies such as South Carolina, where slaves made up 60 percent of the population.

Protecting children during the war also fell to women when men were away. One major concern of Patriot families was that their daughters would fall in love with British officers quartered in their homes. Rebecca Motte was so afraid of this happening that she kept her daughters hidden away in the attic of her house in Charleston the entire time the officers lived in her home—almost two years!

When fighting armies approached, women had little choice but to flee with their children, and different groups chose different sites. Patriots in cities moved in with friends and relatives in the country, as did the Wisters. Patriots on the frontier usually fled to nearby army forts when Loyalists and their Iroquois allies attacked. Eventually the Indian attacks became so menacing that the colonies sent soldiers to the frontier to put an end to the Iroquois threat. Indian women then gathered their children and fled westward toward what is now Buffalo, New York. Loyalists usually fled the colonies or sought shelter behind British lines. They sailed to England or Canada, moved to wilderness areas of what is now Florida and Mississippi, or headed to British-occupied cities. None found the trek toward safety easy no matter which site was chosen.

Patriot Hannah Winthrop and her family sought shelter when the British and Patriots clashed near Cambridge, Massachusetts. After a frightening night of seeing the number of British troops increase dramatically, Hannah decided that her family had to leave Cambridge. She described not only their flight but also that of many other women and their families in a letter she wrote to her dear friend, Mercy Warren:

> After dinner we set out, not knowing whither we went. We were directed to a place called Fresh Pond, about a mile from the town; but what a distressed house did we find there, filled with women whose husbands were gone to meet the assailants; seventy or eighty of these with numbers of infant children crying and agonizing for the fate of their husbands!
>
> Daylight . . . [brought] us news that it [was] useless to return to Cambridge, as the enemy were advancing up the river and firing on the town. To stay in this place was impractical. . . . We began our pilgrimage [to Andover, twenty miles away] alternately walking and riding, the roads filled with frightened women and children, some in carts with their tattered furniture, others on foot fleeing into the woods.[8]

Mary Jemison and the Seneca Home Front

In 1758, fifteen-year-old Mary Jemison (c. 1742–1833) was taken captive in her Pennsylvania cabin by a raiding party of Frenchmen and Shawnee Indians. Shortly after, she was given to the Senecas, members of the Iroquois Confederacy, with whom she spent the rest of her life, eventually marrying one of the tribe's bravest warriors, Hiokatoo.

During the American Revolution, the Senecas sided with the British. Mary's husband was a member of the raiding parties, and Mary helped by providing food for the warriors as well as for Loyalists who joined the raids. Raiding parties did so much damage that the Continental Congress asked General Washington to take action. He ordered General John Sullivan to destroy Iroquois settlements and capture as many prisoners as possible to be held as hostages.

As soon as the Senecas learned that Sullivan was nearby, they met to decide what they should do. In an interview many years later, Mary related her tribe's decision:

> Our [warriors] . . . finally came to the conclusion that they were not strong enough to [stop Sullivan] nor to prevent his taking possession of their fields. . . . The women and children were then sent on towards Buffalo . . . accompanied by part of the [warriors]. . . .
>
> In one or two days . . . Sullivan and his army arrived at Genesee [where I lived], where they destroyed every article of food that they could lay their hands on. A part of our corn they burnt, and threw the remainder into the river. They burnt our houses, killed what few cattle and horses they could find, destroyed our fruit trees, and left nothing but the bare soil and [woods]. . . . [When we returned] . . . there was not a mouthful of any kind of sustenance left, not even enough to keep a child one day from perishing with hunger.[9]

Loyalist women also found the trip to safety difficult, and they often found living conditions in their havens of safety less than ideal. The number of Loyalists who fled was far greater than the British had anticipated, and the army was not adequately prepared to help them. This was especially true in refugee camps in or near British-held cities such as New York, Savannah, and Charleston.

The refugee camp at Charleston was typical. By the end of 1781, more than two hundred Loyalists were dying each day from disease and sheer exhaustion. More than half of the dead were children. The fact that the British had suffered heavy losses that year weighed heavily on the refugees' minds, for many now believed that the Patriots would win the war, and the Loyalists lived in great fear, wondering what would happen to them as a result.

Because most Loyalists had had no time to sell their property or possessions before fleeing, most arrived in the Charleston camp with little money in their pockets. As one observer noted, "After their arrival in Charleston, they built themselves huts [near] the lines, which was called Rawdontown; many of these unfortunate women and children, who lived comfortable at their own homes near Camden [South Carolina], died for want in those miserable huts."[10]

Meanwhile, inside the city, Patriot women continued to rankle their captors. One British soldier in Charleston said in May 1781:

> Even in their dresses the females seem to bid us defiance; . . . they wear their own homespun manufactures and take care to have in their breast knots, and even on their shoes, something that resembles their flag of the thirteen stripes. An officer told Lord Cornwallis not long ago, that he believed if we had destroyed all the men in North America, we should have enough to do to conquer the women. I am heartily tired of this country, and wish myself home.[11]

This British soldier was about to get his wish, for the end of the war was at hand.

Afterword

★

America is not the same.
The very climate seems changed.

Grace Galloway, Loyalist's wife

In early 1781, the British Army was divided into two groups. One group, under Sir Henry Clinton, occupied New York City; the other, under Lord Charles Cornwallis, was in Virginia. Even though Cornwallis was encountering great difficulty from local militiamen and Continental regiments, he still believed that if he had a few more troops the British could gain control over the South and end the rebellion. Cornwallis then asked Clinton to leave New York and join him in Virginia.

While Cornwallis awaited Clinton's reply, he moved all of his troops closer to the coast, where he thought they could easily be picked up by British transport ships if the Patriots' threat became any greater. He selected Yorktown, located on the tip of a peninsula, as his gathering point. Shortly after, close to seven thousand British soldiers massed there.

As soon as General Washington learned that Cornwallis was moving to Yorktown, he put in place a plan that would lead to a stunning victory for the Patriots. This plan relied on three groups: French sailors, local militias, and the Continental Army. The French had joined the Patriot cause in 1778 and had supplied the Continental Army with money, arms, and volunteers, as well as a naval fleet. Now this fleet was to head to Virginia and take control of the colony's coastline, a task the sailors completed by September 5. This meant that the British soldiers gathered at Yorktown could no longer leave by sea.

At the same time, local militias and Continental soldiers in the area were told to form a long line across the neck of the peninsula. Although this line was thinly manned at first, the Patriots were supposed to try to prevent any withdrawal of British soldiers from Yorktown by land.

When Washington arrived in mid-September, bringing with him as many soldiers as he could spare from the New York area, he fortified this line, and by the end of September more than 16,000 soldiers stood between the British and the mainland. Using seventy cannons, the Patriots pounded the British troops, who had little choice but to surrender.

Lord Cornwallis was so ashamed of his loss—to men he considered to be the lowest class of human beings, rabble!—that he would not meet the enemy or personally surrender his sword. Instead, he sent General Charles O'Hara in his place. O'Hara was not any happier about the loss, and he shed tears as he gave up his weapons, according to camp follower Sarah Osborn, who had marched south from New York with Washington and witnessed the surrender:

> [I] stood on one side of the road and the American officers upon the other side when the British officers . . . delivered up [their swords, which I think] were returned again. The British officers rode before the [troops], who marched out beating and playing a melancholy tune ["The World Turned Upside Down"], their drums covered with black handkerchiefs and their fifes with black ribbons tied around them. [They marched] into an old field, and there [put

down] their arms and then returned into town again to await their destiny. . . . The British general at the head of the army was a large, portly man, full face, and the tears rolled down his cheeks as he passed along.[1]

Reactions to Cornwallis's defeat varied in Britain. When word about the surrender reached Lord North, the British prime minister, he at first was too stunned to speak. He realized that Cornwallis's defeat meant that the fighting would have to come to an end, since there were not enough troops to continue the war. North then paced about wildly, throwing his arms into the air, shouting "Oh, God! it is all over!"[2] King George, on the other hand, insisted that the war continue, but how he planned to fight it is not clear. Parliament, like North, believed that the end was at hand, and saw little choice but to negotiate a peace treaty.

On November 30, 1782, a treaty was drawn up and signed by representatives from Great Britain and the colonies who met in Paris, France. This agreement, the Treaty of Paris, was ratified by the Second Continental Congress the following April.

As soon as it was certain that the war was over, the British began to make plans to remove their troops, camp followers, and the last of the Loyalists who wished to leave the colonies or thought it too dangerous to remain. A special invitation was even issued to the Loyalists who had fled to Florida and Mississippi. Historians estimate that 100,000 Loyalists (out of a white population of two million colonists) fled from the colonies as a result of the Revolution, and a little over half of these left with the British when they withdrew their troops from the last two cities they held in the war, New York and Charleston.

When Loyalists had first left the colonies, many did so to find temporary shelter, hoping to return to the colonies if the British were victorious. Now, they knew that their exile was to be permanent, and they had to seek a new home. Almost all of them settled in England, the British West Indies, or Canada.

Those who moved to England were not well received. The English looked down on the newcomers, regarding them as quitters (especially the Loyalists who left the colonies early in the war) and losers. The contempt Loyalists encountered was especially irksome to those who had held important positions in the colonies. To make matters worse, these Americans missed their homeland. Governor Thomas Hutchinson, the last royal governor of Massachusetts, spoke for many when he said he would "rather die in a little country farmhouse in New England than in the best nobleman's seat" in England.[3]

Among the Loyalists in England were Flora MacDonald, who had once raised troops for the king, and Ann Bates, the spy. Flora, who sought safety first in New York, then Canada, spent about eight months in England before moving to Scotland, where she had been born.

Ann Bates spent most of her years in England in poverty, pleading for the money the government had promised her for risking her life during the war. She became bitter over the years, but no less feisty. In a fit of anger, she wrote a letter to British officials. She thought that they were even more contemptible than the rebels, who never would have sunk so low as to abandon her if she had helped them instead. She said, "Haid I Doon half as much for the Scruff of Mankind, I mean the Rabls, I Should not be thus Left to Parish. Was I in Amarica Now to share the same fate of my Noble Unfortunate frind Major André [who was hanged]—it would be much better for me than to Draw out a life Which all Laws, humain and Divine, forbid me to Putt [an end] too."[4]

Loyalists who went to the British West Indies had an easier life than did those in England. Most were slave owners who were allowed to bring their slaves to the islands. About 18,000 Loyalists moved to the British West Indies, and were given large parcels of land by the British government. Each head of family received 40 acres (16 hectares) as well as an additional 20 acres (8 hectares) for each family member and each slave the Loyalist owned. With the help of their slaves, the former colonists cleared their land and built new homes, and although they had to work hard in the beginning, they eventually established thriving communities.

The city of Halifax, in the Canadian province of Nova Scotia, was a destination for many Loyalists from Boston at the end of the Revolution, including Margaret Draper, the newspaper publisher.

By far, the vast majority of Loyalists and former slaves who had been granted freedom when they reached British lines went to Canada, settling primarily in what are now the provinces of Nova Scotia, New Brunswick, and Prince Edward Island. The first Loyalists to go to Canada were 1,100 New Englanders who went to Halifax, Nova Scotia, with British General William Howe when he left Boston in 1776. This group included Margaret Draper, the newspaper publisher. The last Loyalists to reach Canada, a group of about 35,000, did so in the autumn of 1783, when snow already covered the ground. Even though the British government had granted each family that agreed to settle in Canada 500 acres (200 hectares) tax-free for ten years, and provided tools and food, these settlers had to survive a very difficult first winter, most of it spent in tents.

Eleven-year-old Hannah Ingraham of Albany, New York, described her family's experiences, which were not so different from those of other families:

Father said we were to go to [Canada], that a ship was ready to take us there, so we made all haste to get ready.

We had five wagon loads carried down the Hudson [River] in a sloop and then we went on board the transport that was to bring us to Saint John [New Brunswick]. . . . It was the last transport of the season and had on board all those who could not [leave] sooner. . . . This was the last of September. . . . There were no deaths on board, but several babies were born.

It was a sad, sick time after we landed in Saint John. We had to live in tents. The government gave them to us and rations, too. It was just at the first snow then, and the melting snow and the rain would soak up into our beds as we lay. Mother got so chilled and developed rheumatism and was never well afterwards.

[Later we went] up the river in a schooner and were nine days getting to St. Anne's. . . . We lived in a tent at St. Anne's until Father got a house ready.

One morning when we awoke, we found the snow lying deep on the ground all around us. Then Father came wading through it and told us the house was ready and not to stop to light a fire and not to mind the weather, but follow his tracks through the trees. . . . It was snowing fast and oh, so cold. Father carried a chest and we all took something and followed him up the hill.

There was no floor laid, no windows, no chimney, no door, but we had a roof. . . . We toasted bread [around a small fire] and all sat around and ate our breakfast that morning. Mother said . . . "This is the sweetest meal I ever tasted for many a day."[5]

Former slaves who moved to Canada (about three thousand altogether, including more than nine hundred women and seven hundred children) did not fare as well as did the Loyalists. The newly freed slaves simply were not given much support. Former slaves who served in the British Army were given fewer than 100 acres (40 hectares) per family, and most of this was not fit for farming. Those who did not serve received only their transport. As a result, many struggled just to eke out a living when they arrived, and when given a chance to move to Sierra Leone in Africa several years later, almost a thousand did so. There, too, they struggled to survive and encountered many problems.

Although living conditions in Canada were very difficult at first, most of the new immigrants survived. Proud of their loyalty, they maintained close ties with each other, and over the years held meetings and conventions. Eventually they decided to proclaim their loyalty by writing "U.E.L" (United Empire Loyalist) after their names, a practice that is still used today by their descendants. And each year, Canadians honor and remember the Loyalists by reenacting the last group's landing in Saint John, a scene that now draws many tourists.

Some Iroquois Indians who helped the British also went to Canada, including Mary Brant. Most, however, remained in their homes. Their tribes were treated as conquered nations, and the new United States laid claim to their lands. Eventually, almost all of the Iroquois tribes were forced to live on reservations near Buffalo, New York, as white settlers moved into the area.

———

While Loyalists struggled to make a new life for themselves in their new homelands, Americans rejoiced in their victory. Celebrations were held throughout the new nation, and General Washington was honored everywhere he went.

Expectations were high, and few who celebrated victory realized how many problems—economic, social, and political—the new nation faced. Although a few individuals, especially those who owned privateers, had made fortunes during the war, most colonists had experienced hard times and the economy was shaky at best. But now that the colonies were free from British control, Americans could seek markets anywhere they chose. They were also able to stop being mostly suppliers of raw materials, as they had been forced to be under the British, and could manufacture whatever they wished. This would make more money for the Americans than the colonial system had, and although it took years to start new industries and develop good markets, the new nation managed to overcome many obstacles, and the economy flourished as a result.

The new Americans also looked at their society and, heady with the idea of freedom and wanting to make themselves different from British society, decided to tear down some of the established social-class barriers. There would be no American royalty, no lords, no dukes or duchesses; instead, all Americans would be equal, at least in theory. This equality, however, did not apply to slaves.

The desire for equality and equal opportunity created a strong demand for education. Because women had sorely felt the lack of education as they tried to run farms and businesses during the war, mothers insisted that their daughters be given a broader education. Private academies for young ladies became commonplace, even though girls were now allowed to attend classes with boys in public schools and receive the same education.

The new nation also needed to create a government. Representatives chosen just for this task started a confederacy. When this government proved to be too weak to deal with the many problems the new nation faced, another group of representatives devised a federal form of government based on the U.S. Constitution, which was ratified and put into operation in 1789.

While men argued about how representatives should be elected under the Constitution, women again made their plea to be allowed to vote. One proposal debated by the representatives would have allowed single or widowed women who owned property to vote. This did not please Abigail Adams, a tireless advocate for women, who repeatedly urged her husband to remember all the ladies. "I cannot say," she wrote, "that I think you are very generous to the ladies; so whilst you are

The Constitutional Convention was held at Independence Hall in Philadelphia. The Constitution of the United States of America, the document that shaped our nation's government by securing rights for all Americans, was ratified here in 1789.

proclaiming peace and good will to men, [freedom] for all nations, you insist on retaining an absolute power over wives."[6]

Although women would not be given the right to vote for more than 125 years, their lives did change as a result of their participation in the war. This was especially true for those who served on the battlefield. Deborah Sampson, who married Benjamin Gannett shortly after the war, toured the East Coast, giving dramatic readings as well as brief speeches about her adventures in the army. She wore a Continental soldier's uniform while talking about her wartime experiences, a practice that would have caused outrage before the war. Half-soldiers Molly Hays and Molly Corbin and camp follower Sarah Osborn applied for the extension of their husband's army pensions when their husbands died. These women based their claims upon their *own* service during the war as well as their husbands' service, and all three received recognition and financial compensation for the part they played in the war.

Women who entered the political arena during the war remained there. Abigail Adams became even more interested in political issues when her husband was elected the second president of the United States. (Her son, John Quincy Adams, became America's sixth president; however, Abigail did not live to see him inaugurated.) Mercy Warren continued to write, tackling a project that took her more than twenty-five years to complete: a history of the Revolution in three volumes titled *History of the Rise, Progress and Termination of the American Revolution, interspersed with Biographical and Moral Observations*. This obviously very serious scholarly work was published in 1805 under Mercy's name—no more anonymous works for her.

Not all women's lives changed as dramatically as did some of the most active participants of the war. However, though most women went back to their household tasks—even spies like Lydia Darragh and Sally Townsend—their beliefs about themselves and their abilities had changed as a result of the experiences they had during the war.

More confident than ever before, American women in general refused to accept the passive role that colonial women had once been expected to play, and they encouraged their daughters to do likewise. Many women actually discussed what a woman's role should be, trying to determine for themselves how they should live, especially as more and more of them became better educated. Some women spoke out against social codes that said wives had to obey their husbands. Others, such as Judith Sargent Murray, wrote essays, trying to convince Americans that women deserved to have the same rights that men enjoyed. In short, the remarkable women of the Revolution not only made significant contributions to the war for independence, but they also laid the groundwork for yet another revolution—equal rights for women.

TIMELINE

1774   First Continental Congress meets in September.
Penelope Barker drafts the Edenton Proclamation in October.

1775   Mercy Warren publishes "The Group" in April.
The first battles of the war take place at Lexington and Concord, Massachusetts, in April.
The Second Continental Congress meets in May. It takes control of the army, which begins to form near Boston, and appoints George Washington commander in chief.
The colonists surrender Bunker Hill in June. They then lay siege to Boston, Massachusetts, to try to force the British to leave.
The Continental Army, fearing an attack from Canada, a British colony, attacks Canada first. The Continental Army reaches Quebec in September, where it is later defeated.

1776   Flora MacDonald recruits soldiers for King George in January.
The British are forced to withdraw from Boston in March, and Margaret Draper shuts down her Loyalist newspaper and leaves with the British.
The colonies declare independence from Great Britain in July.
The British take control of New York City in late August.
Mary Brant persuades four of the six Iroquois tribes to support the British in September.
Molly Corbin is wounded at Fort Washington in November.
General Washington captures Trenton, New Jersey, which is a major morale booster for the army, in December.

1777   Mary Katherine Goddard publishes the first copy of the Declaration of Independence that includes the names of the signers in January.

Sybil Ludington musters the militia near Danbury, Connecticut, in April.

The British take Philadelphia, Pennsylvania, the Patriots' capital, in September.

The British lose heavily at Saratoga, New York, in October. More than six thousand British and Hessian soldiers are taken prisoner. Baroness von Riedesel becomes a prisoner of war.

Lydia Darragh delivers a warning to General Washington in December.

1778   France enters the war on the side of the Patriots in February.

Molly Hays participates in the Battle at Monmouth Courthouse in June.

Grace Galloway begins her struggle to hold on to her property in July.

1779   Ann Bates begins to spy for the British in January.

British troops leave Philadelphia in June to fortify New York City.

The British turn their attention to the southern colonies where they believe they have strong support from Loyalists. The British take Savannah, Georgia, in December. The Americans try to recapture Savannah for almost a year. They fail.

1780   Charleston, South Carolina, is taken by the British in May.

Esther Reed begins her fund drive for the Continental Army in May.

Sarah Osborn becomes a camp follower in December.

1781   British forces under Lord Cornwallis surrender at Yorktown, Virginia, in September.

1782   Deborah Sampson enlists in the Continental Army in June.

The Treaty of Paris, which grants the colonies independence, is signed by delegates in November.

1783   The Treaty of Paris is ratified by Congress in April.

The British free the rest of their prisoners in New York and Charleston and leave both cities in November.

NOTES

CHAPTER ONE

1. Linda Grant DePauw, *Founding Mothers: Women in America in the Revolutionary Era* (Boston: Houghton Mifflin Company, 1975), p. 49.
2. Mary Beth Norton, *Liberty's Daughters: The Revolutionary Experience of American Women 1750–1800* (Boston: Little, Brown and Company, 1980), p. 11.
3. Selma R. Williams, *Demeter's Daughters: The Women Who Founded America 1587–1787* (New York: Atheneum, 1976), p. 181.
4. Norton, p. 157.

CHAPTER TWO

1. Selma R. Williams, *Demeter's Daughters: The Women Who Founded America 1587–1787* (New York: Atheneum, 1976), p. 271.
2. John C. Dann, editor, *The Revolution Remembered: Eyewitness Accounts of the War for Independence* (Chicago: University of Chicago Press, 1977), pp. 242–244.
3. Elizabeth Evans, *Weathering the Storm: Women of the American Revolution* (New York: Charles Scribner's Sons, 1975), p. 11.
4. Linda Grant DePauw, *Founding Mothers: Women in America in the Revolutionary Era* (Boston: Houghton Mifflin Company, 1975), p. 181.
5. Baroness von Riedesel, *Journal and Correspondence of a Tour of Duty 1776–1783*, translated by Marvin L. Brown, Jr., and Marta Huth (Chapel Hill: University of North Carolina, 1965), pp. 50–52.
6. Baroness von Riedesel, pp. 63, 64.

CHAPTER THREE

1. John Bakeless, *Turncoats, Traitors and Heroes* (New York: J.B. Lippincott Company, 1959), p. 220.

2. Elisabeth Anthony Dexter, *Colonial Women of Affairs: Women in Business and the Professions in America Before 1776* (New York: Houghton Mifflin Company, 1931), p. 73.
3. Elizabeth Evans, *Weathering the Storm: Women of the American Revolution* (New York: Charles Scribner's Sons, 1975), p. 284.
4. Linda Grant DePauw, *Founding Mothers: Women in America in the Revolutionary Era* (Boston: Houghton Mifflin Company, 1975), p. 137.
5. DePauw, p. 138.
6. Bakeless, p. 254.
7. Bakeless, p. 257.

Chapter Four

1. Mary Beth Norton, *Liberty's Daughters: The Revolutionary Experience of American Women 1750–1800* (Boston: Little, Brown and Company, 1980), p. 170.
2. Norton, pp. 188, 189.
3. Selma R. Williams, *Demeter's Daughters: The Women Who Founded America 1587–1787* (New York: Atheneum, 1976), p. 304.
4. Williams, pp. 304, 305.
5. Henry Steele Commager and Richard B. Morris, editors, *The Spirit of 'Seventy-Six* (New York: Harper & Row, 1967), p. 137.
6. Barbara Graymont, *The Iroquois in the American Revolution* (Syracuse, NY: Syracuse University Press, 1972), p. 159.

Chapter Five

1. Mary Beth Norton, *Liberty's Daughters: The Revolutionary Experience of American Women 1750–1800* (Boston: Little, Brown and Company, 1980), p. 180.
2. Norton, p. 181.
3. Linda Grant DePauw, *Founding Mothers: Women in America in the Revolutionary Era* (Boston: Houghton Mifflin Company, 1975), p. 165.

Chapter Six

1. Richard M. Dorson, editor, *American Rebels: Personal Narratives of the American Revolution* (New York: Pantheon Books, 1953), pp. 220, 221.

2. Mary Beth Norton, *Liberty's Daughters: The Revolutionary Experience of American Women 1750–1800* (Boston: Little, Brown and Company, 1980), p. 203.
3. Norton, p. 208.
4. Norton, pp. 204, 205.
5. Elizabeth Evans, *Weathering the Storm: Women of the American Revolution* (New York: Charles Scribner's Sons, 1975), pp. 124, 125.
6. Evans, p. 191.
7. Selma R. Williams, *Demeter's Daughters: The Women Who Founded America 1587–1787* (New York: Atheneum, 1976), pp. 256, 257.
8. Williams, p. 273.
9. June Namias, editor, *A Narrative of the Life of Mrs. Mary Jemison* (Norman: University of Oklahoma Press, 1992), pp. 104, 105.
10. Robert Stansbury Lambert, *South Carolina Loyalists in the American Revolution* (Columbia: University of South Carolina Press, 1989), p. 227.
11. Frank Moore, compiler, *The Diary of the American Revolution 1775–1781* (New York: Washington Square Press, 1967), pp. 506, 507.

CHAPTER SEVEN

1. John C. Dann, editor, *The Revolution Remembered: Eyewitness Accounts of the War for Independence* (Chicago: University of Chicago Press, 1977), p. 245.
2. John Miller, *Triumph of Freedom 1775–1783* (Boston: Little, Brown and Company, 1948), p. 612.
3. Donald Chidsey, *The Loyalists: The Story of Those Americans Who Fought Against Independence* (New York: Crown Publishers, Inc., 1973), p. 176.
4. John Bakeless, *Turncoats, Traitors and Heroes* (New York: J.B. Lippincott Company, 1959), p. 361.
5. Catherine S. Crary, editor, *The Price of Loyalty: Tory Writings from the Revolutionary Era* (New York: McGraw-Hill Book Company, 1973), p. 402.
6. Emily Taft Douglas, *Remember the Ladies: The Story of Great Women Who Helped Shape America* (New York: G.P. Putnam's Sons, 1966), p. 51.

BIBLIOGRAPHY

Bakeless, John. *Turncoats, Traitors and Heroes.* Philadelphia: J.B. Lippincott Company, 1959.

Blumenthal, Walter Hart. *Women Camp Followers of the American Revolution.* New York: Arno Press, 1974.

Bologna, Dando. "Sybil Ludington: The Colonel's Daring Daughter." *The Sunday Republican Magazine* (February 16, 1975): 3–5.

Brown, Wallace. *The Good Americans.* New York: William Morrow, 1969.

Chidsey, Donald Barr. *The Loyalists: The Story of Those Americans Who Fought Against Independence.* New York: Crown Publishers, Inc., 1973.

Claghorn, Charles E. *Women Patriots of the American Revolution: A Biographical Dictionary.* Metuchen, NJ: The Scarecrow Press, Inc., 1991.

Commager, Henry Steele, and Richard B. Morris, editors. *The Spirit of 'Seventy-Six: The Story of the American Revolution as Told by Participants.* New York: Harper & Row, 1967.

Crary, Catherine S., editor. *The Price of Loyalty: Tory Writings from the Revolutionary Era.* New York: McGraw-Hill Book Company, 1973.

Dann, John C. *The Revolution Remembered: Eyewitness Accounts of the War for Independence.* Chicago: University of Chicago Press, 1977.

Darragh, Henry. "Lydia Darragh of the Revolution." *The Pennsylvania Magazine of History and Biography* 23 (1899): 86–91.

DePauw, Linda Grant. *Founding Mothers: Women in America in the Revolutionary Era.* Boston: Houghton Mifflin Company, 1975.

Dexter, Elisabeth Anthony. *Colonial Women of Affairs: Women in Business and the Professions in America Before 1776.* Boston: Houghton Mifflin Company, 1931.

————. *Career Women of America 1776–1840*. Francestown, NH: Marshall Jones Company, 1950.

Douglas, Emily Taft. *Remember the Ladies: The Story of Great Women Who Helped Shape America*. New York: G.P. Putnam's Sons, 1966.

Engle, Paul. *Women in the American Revolution*. Chicago: Follett Publishing Company, 1976.

Evans, Elizabeth. *Weathering the Storm: Women of the American Revolution*. New York: Charles Scribner's Sons, 1975.

Graymont, Barbara. *The Iroquois in the American Revolution*. Syracuse, NY: Syracuse University Press, 1972.

Lambert, Robert S. *South Carolina Loyalists in the American Revolution*. Columbia: University of South Carolina Press, 1989.

Miller, John. *Triumph of Freedom 1775–1783*. Boston: Little, Brown and Company, 1948.

Moore, Frank, compiler, and John Anthony Scott, editor. *The Diary of the American Revolution 1775–1781*. New York: Washington Square Press, 1967.

Norton, Mary Beth. *Liberty's Daughters: The Revolutionary Experience of American Women 1750–1800*. Boston: Little, Brown and Company, 1980.

Seaver, James E. *The Narrative of the Life of Mrs. Mary Jemison*. Edited by June Namias. Norman: University of Oklahoma Press, 1992.

Sherr, Lynn, and Jurate Kazickas. *The American Women's Gazetteer*. New York: Bantam Books, 1976.

Vining, Elizabeth Gray. *Flora: A Biography*. Philadelphia: J.B. Lippincott Company, 1966.

Von Riedesel, Baroness Frederika. *Journal and Correspondence of a Tour of Duty 1776–1783*. Edited and translated by M.L. Brown, Jr., and Marta Huth. Chapel Hill: University of North Carolina Press, 1965.

Williams, Selma R. *Demeter's Daughters: The Women Who Founded America 1587–1787*. New York: Atheneum, 1976.

FURTHER READING

There are few books for young adults devoted entirely to women in the American Revolution. Patricia Edwards Clyne's book, *Patriots in Petticoats* (New York: Dodd, Mead & Company, 1976), is one of the few available, and it has lots of brief sketches of women not mentioned elsewhere. *The American Revolutionaries: A History in Their Own Words 1750–1800*, edited by Milton Meltzer, (New York: Thomas Y. Crowell, 1987), has only a few events as seen through women's eyes. However, one of the excerpts in the book is camp follower Sarah Osborn's story, and this section makes very interesting reading.

Biographies about women mentioned in *Those Remarkable Women of the Revolution* usually contain several chapters about the subjects' lives during the war. *Abigail Adams: Witness to a Revolution* by Natalie Bober (New York: Atheneum Books for Young Readers, 1995) examines the life of one of the most outspoken women of the era, while *Deborah Sampson: Soldier of the Revolution* by Harold Felton (New York: Dodd, Mead & Company, 1976) examines the life of one of the most active women of the conflict. *George and Martha Washington at Home in New York* by Beatrice Siegel (New York: Four Winds, 1989) briefly discusses Martha's involvement in the war before turning to her life after the Revolution. In addition, a book about Mary Jemsion, *Captured by Indians: The Life of Mary Jemison* (North Haven, CT: Linnet Books, 1995) contains a chapter about her life with the Seneca Indians during the war. Mary told her story to James Weaver, who recorded and published the narrative in 1828. This book is an edited version for young adults.

Cobblestone, a history magazine for young readers, which many libraries carry, explores a different historical theme each month. For more information about the Revolution and some of its female participants, check out *Cobblestone* articles "American Revolution Tales" (September 1983), "British Loyalists" (August 1987), "First Ladies of the White House" (March 1992), and "The Adams Family" (November 1993).

INDEX

Page numbers in *italics* refer to illustrations.